CHASING SKINNY RABBITS

Other Books by or Coauthored by John Trent

CHASING SKINNY RABBITS

JOHN TRENT, PHD

THOMAS NELSON
Since 1798

NASHVILLE DALLAS MEXICO CITY RIO DE JANEIRO BEIJING

Chasing Skinny Rabbits provides information of a general nature and is not to be used as an alternative method for conditions requiring the services of a personal physician or other health-care professional.

Information contained in this book or in any other publication, article, or Web site should not be considered a substitute for consultation with a board-certified doctor to address individual medical needs. Individual facts and circumstances will determine the treatment that is most appropriate. The *Chasing Skinny Rabbits* publisher and its author, John Trent, PhD, disclaim any liability, loss, or damage that may result in the implementation of the contents of this book.

Published in Nashville, Tennessee, by Thomas Nelson. Thomas Nelson is a trademark of Thomas Nelson, Inc.

Thomas Nelson, Inc. titles may be purchased in bulk for educational, business, fund-raising, or sales promotional use. For information, please e-mail SpecialMarkets@ThomasNelson.com.

Unless otherwise noted, Scripture quotations are taken from the Holy Bible, New International Version®. ©1973, 1978, 1984 by International Bible Society. Used by permission of Zondervan Bible Publishing House. All rights reserved.

Scripture quotations noted NASB are taken from the New American Standard Bible®, © 1960, 1962, 1963, 1968, 1971, 1972, 1973, 1975, 1977, 1995 by The Lockman Foundation. Used by permission.

Page Design by Casey Hooper

Library of Congress Cataloging-in-Publication Data
Trent, John T.
  Chasing skinny rabbits : what leads you into emotional and spiritual exhaustion—and what can lead you out / John Trent.
    p. cm.
  Includes bibliographical references.
  ISBN 978-0-7852-9784-0 (hardcover)

  1. Christian life. I. Title.
  BV4501.3.T7325 2007
  248.4—dc22

                                                                2007030144

Printed in the United States of America
07 08 09 10 QW 5 4 3 2 1

This book is dedicated to my wife, Cindy, and to our daughters, Kari and Laura. All three do a great job of keeping me real and aren't afraid to speak up if they see me chasing after Skinny Rabbits. May each of their paths always be blessed and ever lead toward God's best—and away from Skinny Rabbit Trails!

CONTENTS

CONTENTS

ACKNOWLEDGMENTS

While any honest acknowledgments could go on for pages, I'd like to give special thanks to five people who had an important part in shaping and taking this book on Skinny Rabbits seriously. The first two are publishers Byron Williamson and Joey Paul, for first sharing with me the idea that came to be called *Chasing Skinny Rabbits*. To John Fornof and Cedric Hornstadt, deepest thanks are due as well; to John for sharing his award-winning skills as a screenwriter to make characters in this book come alive, and for Cedric's outstanding drawing skills that have done a wonderful job of capturing Skinny Rabbits in art for this book and our Skinny Rabbit E-mail Alert—available to send to a friend or family member whom you think is chasing a Skinny Rabbit at www.StrongFamilies.com or www.skinnyrabbits.com. Thanks are due as well to my very patient and professional book agent, Lee Hough, at Alive Communications. He has been a loyal friend for almost three decades and a wise and greatly valued counselor when it comes to all things books for almost a decade. My deepest thanks to all these and to all who, for sake of space, go unnamed.

1
BEWARE THE
SKINNY RABBIT!

The bravest and strongest hunters of the village gathered by the flickering embers of the campfire. Their dogs lay quietly nearby, dreaming of the hunt to come. The magnificent Great Stag had been seen again. Farmers had spotted the immense creature standing proudly high on the crags. Travelers caught glimpses of it bounding through the woods. Women and children insisted they had seen a grand, noble animal that looked like an enormous deer disappearing into the morning fog or standing at the edge of a field at twilight. What's more, they had found its tracks—huge prints in plowed fields or in rain-washed roads. Yes, there was no doubt about it; the Great Stag was on the move.

THE HUNT FOR THE GREAT STAG

Each hunter gazed into the fire, his eyes gleaming not only with firelight but also with hope. Each prayed it would be his dogs that found the trail of the Great Stag and that his eyes would be the first to catch sight of the creature. They hunted this Stag not to kill the magnificent animal, for it was told that to the one who captured it alive would pass down power, insight, and untold wealth fit to benefit generations.

In the morning a battle cry arose from the mighty men. Quickly they gathered their kit, mounted their mighty steeds, and swept into the forest. On and on they rode, through wilderness and forest, over hill and dale, through stream and glade, hounds baying in the excitement of the chase.

For days and days the hunt went on. At times the hunters grew weary, but each new sighting of the Great Stag's tracks renewed their energy. The Great Stag was elusive, and they knew the chase would not be easy. But the prize was worth every effort, so they pressed on.

After many days of trekking through bush and briar, the dogs were tired, and the hunters were dog-tired. All were famished. Their food supply was diminishing, and daily rations had become too meager to fill the gnawing emptiness in their bellies. Nonetheless, before the morning fog had lifted the next day, the men mounted and took up their chase.

With the hunting dogs far in front, one man in the middle of the pack of hunters glimpsed something moving to his right. Something moving swiftly through the fog. Surely it was the Great Stag! He spurred his mount, moving quickly away from the others, and soon spotted the movement again. Each time he was ready to give up the chase, there came a flash of movement that spurred him on again. The hunter followed doggedly, going deeper and deeper into the unknown forest, farther and farther away from his companions. At last, his persistence paid off. He had run his foe into a narrow box canyon. Finally, his prey was right in front of him! But instead of the Great Stag . . . it was a rabbit. A Skinny Rabbit at that.

Exhilaration turned to exhaustion for the Hunter. The long-eared creature that had drawn him so far off course was only now shown to be unworthy of the chase. This rabbit was thin as a hemlock twig, and its scrawny bones had no meat on them. The warrior turned away in disappointment and disgust and swung wearily into his saddle. He had wasted his time and much-needed energy, and by following a rabbit trail instead of the real trail, he had fallen far behind his companions.

He reined his horse around to retrace his steps. But he found no trace of his trail in the brush and briars. He tried his best to remember the path, but soon to his dismay, he realized it was hopeless. He had been so intent on chasing the Skinny Rabbit that he had lost his bearings, cut himself off from the other hunters, and totally lost the trail of the Great Stag.

Darkness descended into the forest. Ominous yellow eyes glowed from the brushes, and menacing growls chilled his bones. He dared not stop but wandered through the trees and brush, hoping somehow to find his companions or pick up the trail of the Great Stag. Soon the ground began to slope downward, leading the warrior to hope he was approaching a stream he might follow out of the forest. He spurred his horse forward, but instead of water he found himself mired in a thick bog, so deep his horse could no longer lift its feet.

The warrior hung his head in despair. Not only had he lost his way; not only had he wasted valuable time and energy; not only was he exhausted; but he knew he had lost his chance to achieve his great goal . . . and would regret it for years to come.

All because he had chased that accursed Skinny Rabbit.

BEWARE SKINNY RABBITS

Beware! There are Skinny Rabbits all around you. They lurk at work and hide in the bushes along your career path. They can lure you away from anything worthy—a great marriage, a career goal, a lifelong friendship. They can wreak havoc in small groups, workplace teams, and even churches. Chasing a Skinny Rabbit does worse than just get you off track; it will lead you further and further down a path that will drain the very life from you—killing your excitement, your creativity, your drive. Skinny Rabbits separate you from your money, kill precious time, and can even destroy your life. And the pursuit of them leaves you exhausted—physically, mentally, emotionally, and finally, spiritually bankrupt—more empty than you ever thought you could possibly be.

The tragedy is that most of us won't realize we're pursuing a Skinny Rabbit until it's too late—until we've lost precious months or even years in the chase. Until it dawns on us that we've lost our chance to catch the Great Stag we set out to find.

A Skinny Rabbit is anything that pulls you away

from a path of purpose and life and leads you into a forest of separation, exhaustion, and even (if you don't stop the chase) the death of a dream, relationship, or chance to reach God's best. It is any pursuit that distracts you from a worthwhile goal that, over time, would lead to great reward for a far lesser one that gives you little but bare bones.

We've all been had, to some degree, by this "wascally wabbit."

Maybe it was that promotion we sought that we just knew would change everything . . . but instead of giving us anything, it took every ounce of our time and energy, nearly ruining our families in the empty pursuit. A Skinny Rabbit may have been that best friend or trusted business partner whom we just knew was leading us to success, only to be left alone and betrayed in the end.

Or a Skinny Rabbit may be that person we've dated for three years who seems so *right* but who still has given no sign of commitment . . . or that car we just had to have that came equipped with every option—including life-draining payments—or that investment opportunity that we just knew was going to triple our money . . . or even that ministry position that held so much promise but left us feeling squeezed out and emotionally discarded like a sour dishrag.

My goal with this book is to help you recognize these Skinny Rabbits and their traps and trails *before* they divert you from better goals and before they lead you to emotional, physical, and even spiritual exhaustion.

I want you—and the people you know best and love most—to know the importance of asking the question, *Is this a Skinny Rabbit?*

> My goal is to motivate you to
> ask the question early and often,
> "Is this a Skinny Rabbit?"

You'll soon see that question is crucial to ask both of the good things that suddenly pop into your life and of those trails you may have been following for years. This book will help you determine whether or not you're on a Skinny Rabbit Trail and will equip you with a Skinny Rabbit Detector, which can be of great practical and immediate help. And perhaps of most benefit, you'll be able to see more clearly those Great Stag opportunities— how to spot real potential to reach the places God intended when He first dreamed of you.

Read on!

2

OUR FIRST LOOK AT THE SKINNY RABBIT

Remember the old Road Runner cartoons? As the
Road Runner rocketed across the desert, the rascally
Coyote zoomed along the highway, close on the bird's
tail—with brand-new rocket skates he had mail-ordered
from Acme Rocket Skate Company. Suddenly, the camera would freeze-frame on the Coyote, and we'd have a
good look at the critter.

To help you identify the Skinny Rabbit in your life,
we're giving you a freeze-frame of this elusive little dis-
tracter. After all, it will help you stay on the right trail
if you can learn to tell the difference between the Great
Stag's tracks and a Skinny Rabbit's. You would think the
differences too obvious to mention, but sometimes our
immediate needs can create illusions, making Skinny
Rabbits appear much larger and tastier than they are.

Skinny Rabbits have been with us for a long time,
almost always quite appealing and offering more than

The Skinny Rabbit

rabbitus skinnius, **n.** Anything that pulls you away from a path of purpose and life and leads you into a wilderness of exhaustion and regret.

they deliver. You'll probably recognize some of the famous Skinny Rabbits in the following list:

The Hare. At the starting line, this Skinny Rabbit looks like the winner already. He starts off in a burst of glory, but he's all show. He's cocky, and he conks out in the long run. The steady, faithful tortoise wins against this blazing bunny of showiness every time.

Br'er Rabbit. It's tempting to take up with this little guy because he seems smart and resourceful. But stick with him, and you'll end up stuck in a tar pit of little white lies with no way to pull yourself out.

The Magician's White Rabbit. This Skinny Rabbit is illusive. He looks appealing, but chase him, and he'll disappear at the drop of a hat.

The White Rabbit in Alice in Wonderland. It's always tempting to follow a critter that seems to be going somewhere. But he's always "late, late, for a very important date," and when you get there, you'll find the door closed and locked.

Peter Rabbit. This Skinny Rabbit looks awfully cute, but follow him and you'll lose more than your jacket and your shoes. You may wind up on Mr. McGregor's trophy wall.

Bugs Bunny. This clever Skinny Rabbit is smart, and it's natural to want to follow someone smart. But chase him and he'll outwit you. "What's up, Doc?" Your blood pressure. Your debt. Your frustration.

Playboy Bunny. This Skinny Rabbit is seductive, seeming to offer mouthwatering pleasure but never telling you the terrible price . . . until you're hooked and your soul is bone-dry.

Energizer Bunny. This Skinny Rabbit keeps going, and going, and going. Question is, *where* is he going? More importantly, where is he taking *you*?

Chasing a Skinny Rabbit is actually quite exhilarating. It's the blur of the fur, the thrill of anticipation, the dream of the quick fix. But it's a mad dash to oblivion. Because once you finally catch the Skinny Rabbit, you'll see that it has nothing to offer that is worth the effort. And to make matters worse, you'll find yourself far off the road you intended to travel. In fact, that's the time when most people realize they've made a big mistake. When they're isolated and alone and full of regret and sorrow over how much time and life they've wasted . . . not to mention the people they've hurt.

o o o

Let's bring the concept of the Skinny Rabbit home, specifically into the workplace, by looking at Don. Don was on a solid career track with a company in his chosen field when he met Jerry, who quickly became Don's best friend and offered Don a chance to *partner* with him and go out on their own.

As the months went by, Don's wife, Mary, warned him many times about Jerry, and Don was sick and tired of it. After all, Jerry had reached out to *him*, opened up doors that moved his career forward in leaps. Jerry made him a partner in all they were doing. Okay, they'd never actually *signed* the partnership documents, but Jerry had introduced him as his partner a hundred times. Mary was just being her usual paranoid self, seeing problems where there were actually awesome opportunities.

Of course, Don was the one working all those extra hours during the week and almost every weekend while Jerry was always out doing his thing and spending time with his family. And there were all those promises that hadn't been followed up on yet. Promises of pay increases and time off and getting some credit of his own. But Jerry was *busy*, after all. And what went around would certainly come around.

Don had been there for Jerry and his family countless times when they needed him (from finishing major projects with Jerry's name alone emblazoned on them, to dog-sitting countless times, to taking Jerry's son to the hospital to get stitches when Jerry was out of town). But payback was coming. It was only a matter of time before Mary would have to eat her nay-saying words and abandon her baseless concerns.

Instead, it was Don who had to swallow the news that Jerry had sold the company (sold *their* company!) and was moving it and his family out of state. It would be forty-five days from the time Don heard of the sale until Jerry, his family, and the business would be *gone*. And while Don was told that he could work for full pay right up to the day they left (Jerry wanted to be *fair*, after all), the new owners rejected any severance for Don because of all the moving costs for Jerry and the office.

And, of course, moving Don and his family to Aspen with him would be out of the question, Jerry explained. The new company had "their own people" to work with Jerry now. People that could really make Jerry's dreams come true.

Ten years of working his heart out for his *partner* and *their* company . . . dashed in a single harsh day when Don finally woke up and saw whom he'd really been partnered with . . . a Skinny Rabbit.

o o o

Rachel was an intelligent, attractive English teacher in her late twenties who fell in love with Michael about five years ago. Michael was her dream man—tall with long dark hair and an easygoing manner that attracted her the first time he smiled at her. He was deep. They had picnics together by a pond where they actually quoted poetry to each other. He was handsome. He had those rare looks that could turn girls' heads while making men feel that he was a normal guy who would be a great friend. He was the complete package, and they dreamed of a future together—well, at least *she* dreamed.

Michael didn't really have a full-time job. He was a songwriter who played his guitar at whatever restaurant or coffee shop wanted live music around town. He couldn't stand the idea of a regular work schedule. So he lived at home, caring for his ill mother. Perhaps most of

all, this compassion for his mother is what made Rachel
out-of-her-head attracted to Michael.

Although Michael expressed his love for Rachel many
times, he didn't like the idea of getting married "right
now," but for her sake he promised he'd consider it. And
he promised. And promised. And Rachel kept on believ-
ing that this gorgeous, deep, sensitive, compassionate,
artistic man would change. She loved him so much she
was sure he would feel it and come around in time.

But instead of it all coming around, it all came apart.
One night Michael sent Rachel a long e-mail—five
years of relationship boiled down to a few electronic
paragraphs. He wrote her saying he was sorry, but the

relationship had to end. He was worn out from the pressure of marriage hanging over his head. It was affecting his ability to be *creative* and hurting his music. In fact, while it hurt him to say it, it was really *her* fault that his career hadn't taken off. By being so controlling, she had held him back.

That morning, Rachel woke up in more ways than one. Michael was never going to change. He'd never *intended* to change. And she'd spent five years chasing a Skinny Rabbit.

If only the loss of years was the only thing that hurt so much.

Now that Rachel's eyes and mind were open, her memory flashed back to three fine men she'd ignored while pursuing Michael. All three had knocked on her door at one time, but they just didn't measure up to her sweet Michael. One became a famous portrait artist who fell in love and married a Southern belle. One built a solid career in real estate and was now happily married with two kids. And one worked for the State Department, which had sent him to work at the embassy in Italy. Any one of these men would have made a great husband . . . to live with, to laugh with, to enjoy life together. But all of them were gone. Dark waves of regret washed over Rachel's mind. The Great Stags had escaped, and she was left with a deadbeat, Skinny Rabbit drifter named Michael—or now, with nothing but the memory of him.

o o o

Jack was in heaven. Okay, there were no streets of gold. No angels flying around strumming harps. But he was living the dream he'd had since he was a teen. Jack had made it to Hollywood. Well, he hadn't made it *in* Hollywood. Not yet. But at least he'd made it *to* Hollywood. And that was the big step his writing buddies back in Ohio didn't have the guts to make.

Jack's wife, Haley, was the best, and he knew it. She believed in him. In fact, her faith was so solid, she gave up family and friends she had known all her life to make the move with her husband. Their two little kids—

five-year-old Jason and three-year-old Emily—seemed to like their little bungalow in West Hollywood.

Life was good. Well, at least good was on its way. Only, before he knew it, three years of *almost* had gone by. He *almost* got an agent at one point. *Almost* got to talk to a famous movie star about an amazing movie idea he had. *Almost* got his script in front of a major director. (A friend had actually slipped it onto the great man's desk. He was *that close* to being discovered.)

Meantime, Haley worked at a nearby medical clinic. It was two blocks away, so she walked every day to work. That way Jack could drive their beat-up Toyota to his appointments while the kids were in day care.

Yes, Jack was on his way. But not the way he imagined. Haley was burning out, regretting the move. Regretting what this life was doing to the kids. Regretting that she had left her family and everyone and everything she knew and loved. She had asked Jack many times to get a normal day job and pursue his screenwriting dreams either late at night or early in the morning. But he wasn't listening. She made it clear that she wasn't asking him to abandon his dream, just asking him to help out financially because the needs were so great. And she pleaded with him to be there for her and the kids, at least on weekends. But for Jack, taking time off when he was so close to making it made no sense. That's what Skinny Rabbits do—focus us on the mirage in the distance while blinding us to the needs right beside us.

Jack didn't realize it, but it was what he was doing that didn't make sense. When you're chasing a Skinny Rabbit, the true goal filled with real significance and satisfaction can slip away before you know what's happening. Happiness, fulfillment, and deep satisfaction were right there within Jack's reach. While he was grasping for the pot of gold at the end of the rainbow, living treasures of love and deep joy were living right in his very house. Almost four years into his dream, the end of the rainbow still hadn't settled on that house, but the end of Jack's marriage had emptied it. He now drives into what was their family apartment, where Haley, Jason, and Emily, the most important people in his life, used to live. And the Skinny Rabbit is still hopping around out there in Tinseltown.

o   o   o

Yvette was all career. And she loved it. Advertising was a lucrative, fast-moving, exciting business. Especially in Manhattan. But one day Yvette bumped into a friend she hadn't seen in a decade. Liz was pushing a stroller with a little bundle of heaven inside—a little girl with golden curls framing bright blue eyes and chubby little cheeks that just begged to be tweaked.

Something tugged at Yvette's heart. She was thirty-six.

She had already chosen her path. It was rewarding. Fulfilling. Sometime in the future when she left the agency, she would also leave a lasting legacy.

Ha! Who was she fooling? What legacy? Suddenly Yvette realized that idea was strictly a daydream. Advertising was a fast-moving stream. If she stepped out of it, no one would really notice. You don't leave footprints in a stream. People stepped in. People stepped out. But the stream moved on without a care.

Yvette had a routine doctor's exam that afternoon. "Just out of curiosity," she asked her doctor, who was looking over her chart, "what's the average age for a woman to have her first child here in Manhattan?" Without looking up, the doctor replied, "Forty-one."

The doctor was nonchalant, but something inside Yvette was already in motion. That afternoon, she told her boss, "I'm going home."

"Fine," he replied.

"For good," she added.

Yvette had a generous severance package, so she could coast a little while financially. Within months she met a retired airline pilot who had lost his wife to cancer. They fell in love. Now she's mother to a family of six beautiful kids and works part-time with her best friend—another career mom who joined her in launching their own small ad agency. She's not pulling down high-five figures anymore. In fact, she spends many days cleaning up after little hands that have left peanut butter on the walls. But she's happier than she's ever been. Yvette's life is rich and full. It's an excitement of a different sort. It's a feeling of sowing well for the future. And she's never looked back—not once.

Yvette realized the career she was chasing was a Skinny Rabbit. She took decisive action and discovered the real treasure: a life of substance, purpose, and legacy.

O O O

Unlike Don, Rachel, and Jack, Yvette realized before it was too late, before too much was lost, that she was on a Skinny Rabbit Trail. She chose to get off the trail before she was lost in a forest or mired in a bog. In this book I want to help you to be like Yvette. I want to give you the tools to remain sharp, alert, and aware. Rabbit Trails are everywhere, and you don't want any of them to draw you off from your quest for the Great Stag. You never want to settle for less than the best available to you and, certainly, not for less than God can accomplish through you. If, like Yvette, you suddenly wake up to the fact that you're on the wrong trail, it's time to face up to it and admit, in the words of the eloquent Elmer Fudd, *"I'm hunting wabbits!"* Don't waste another moment on that trail. Call off your dogs and turn back to the greater quest.

What are some of these Skinny Rabbit Trails? I'm glad you asked, because that's what I'm going to address in the next chapter.

3
THE MOST COMMON
SKINNY RABBIT TRAILS

To help you realize just how many Skinny Rabbit Trails can lure you from your quest, we're going to turn to Elmer and Eloise Smudley for help. They're a hypothetical couple, but their stories are all too real.

You'd like the Smudleys. Elmer's a regular, likable guy. He's both a talented detail person and a relatable people person. This combination has helped him to work his way up through the ranks of the local pickle factory—Paula's Pickles—where he's been recently promoted to vice president of Pickle Jar Design. His job is to make sure each of Paula's pickles is safe and secure as it travels across the fruited plains of America.

Elmer's wife, Eloise, is a bright and energetic woman with a wonderful gift of compassion. She's very involved in church and volunteer activities. In fact, her social calendar resembles the radar screen of an air traffic controller. For the most part, she keeps events and appointments in the air without collisions or major catastrophes. Most everyone in the neighborhood knows her as Mom, including her two kids, Bobby and Betsy.

Elmer and Eloise are more than a nice couple. They're way above average when it comes to caring for others and in wanting to care for each other and their kids. But they're at serious risk and about to feel the lure of following the rabbit.

As we will see in looking at the Smudleys, it's not just the big temptations that lead us down Skinny Rabbit Trails; it's most often the normal choices in life that we face every day. In this chapter and the next, we'll look at five of the most common Skinny Rabbit Trails. It's amazing how these five trails can quickly branch out to become a spiderweb of dead-end trails—any of which can get you lost or trap you in a bog or pit.

Let's begin by looking from a safe distance at all the misleading trails that pop up in front of the Smudleys, each with its own Skinny Rabbit.

THE ALL-TAKE-AND-NO-GIVE TRAIL

The doorbell rang. Twice. Elmer already knew who it was. Milton was the Smudleys' next-door neighbor who had been "between jobs" for about five years now. And he needed some cash. Again.

Elmer had a soft heart for this guy who had been hit hard in life. He frequently gave Milton money to help him through the tough times, as any good friend would. One time Elmer had suggested that Milton get a job at the local convenience store. He could also work as a security guard; it involved just three hours of sitting in a booth for some pretty good change, plus benefits. Both jobs could help tide Milton over. But he rolled his eyes as if Elmer were explaining something to a dull child. The convenience store and sitting in a security booth just weren't Milton's calling.

What was calling Elmer at the moment was the doorbell. He paused once more and felt guilty about it. He had a lot to do and was half-tempted to pretend he wasn't home. But finally, as always, he opened the door.

Milton was a talker. He would go on and on about how he was actually a blood relative of President Millard Fillmore and why he hated pimento cheese and how his sixth-grade science teacher gave him a blue ribbon for fungus. And, of course, there were the problems with his relatives (ungrateful lot), and at the end of the conversation, there was always the *Ask*.

The Ask was when the tears always came on cue, just before Elmer opened up his wallet to do what he knew was his Christian duty. To help out with the rent or the car payment (a newer car than Elmer's) . . . or to help with the trip Milton just had to make to try and talk some sense into those ungrateful relatives.

Elmer rarely got a word in when Milton was gabbing. By the time Milton left, three hours had evaporated, and Elmer was exhausted. Milton was taking Elmer down a Skinny Rabbit Trail. A trail that was all take and no give—draining life from Elmer.

So is the answer to have a heart of steel when it comes to people in need? Absolutely not. But as we'll see, keeping off of Rabbit Trails means adding wisdom to one's compassion and bringing real life before both the giver and receiver. Milton's tearstained *needs* weren't real at all, and neither man was becoming a better person because of their relationship.

In giving in to Milton, Elmer was being led and drained by an All-Take person. To stay off that Rabbit Trail, he needed to stop giving in to Milton's selfish, woe-is-me pleas. An authentic friendship is one where we have the guts to be real to our friends—to confront them lovingly, to help them grow, which means sometimes not giving them money or helping them to be irresponsible again. Even if it means they have to work at the convenience store or in that security booth. Elmer hadn't confronted Milton yet. He was assisting Milton's demise, not preventing it.

If you're on the All-Take-and-No-Give Skinny Rabbit Trail, you'll find yourself being drained more and more while your friend (or relative) is growing more and more dependent and even less motivated to get moving. In an All-Take relationship neither party gains more purpose or life, and the stage is set for significant losses of all sorts.

Poor Elmer. Milton was just the first of the Rabbit Trails he encountered.

THE POSSESSIONS-THAT-POSSESS-US TRAIL

Elmer almost stared a hole in the page of his newspaper. The headline (so obviously a Skinny Rabbit Trail that you could almost see patches of rabbit fur on it) hooked him right away: "Triple Your Money in Just Three Months!" His imagination carried him away:

I'm in the Bahamas.

No, I'm driving my Lamborghini in the Bahamas.

No, wait. I'm driving my Lamborghini around my private island in the Bahamas.

Elmer read on. A gentleman named Guy Getyours was coming to town for one day only to teach his nationally famous Triple Your Money techniques to a select few. And the seminar was *absolutely free*! Wow! Soon Elmer was no longer imagining. He was now actually *in* the Triple Your Money seminar—on the front row! He took notes on having a positive mental attitude about money, on donating money to charity, and on using money to make dreams happen.

He bought Guy Getyours's best-selling book, *Triple Your Money*, a $150 value, for just $49.99! (It was a special seminar discount for that day only.) He bought Guy Getyours's best-selling curriculum titled Triple Your Money, a $1,200 value, for just $499! (It was a special seminar discount for that day only.) And he bought Guy Getyours's best-selling DVD series titled Triple Your Money, a $3,500 value, for just $2,300! (It was a special seminar discount for that day only). When Elmer added it all up, he had saved over $2,000!

Over the next few days, Elmer read through the best-selling book, took notes on the best-selling curriculum, and watched a couple of the best-selling DVDs. He learned he could make lots of money by setting up seminars called Triple Your Money. At each seminar, Elmer could sell Guy's books and Guy's curriculum products and Guy's DVDs—all of which showed students (privately known as *suckers*) how they in turn could set up Triple Your Money seminars.

All it took was a simple headline to lure Elmer down this Skinny Rabbit Trail. I should note that this Rabbit Trail alone is responsible for the destruction of an incredible number of marriages, not to mention railroad cars full of derailed dreams for the kids in those homes.

But the Smudley family wasn't done with Skinny Rabbit Trails. Elmer was always interested in a "two-fur," and he was about to get it. Eloise was about to find a way to triple the number of possessions their family had without even going to a Guy Getyours seminar.

Eloise spotted *the* dress in the window of the town's most upscale department store, Needless Markup. It was the dress of her dreams—and in her color! In moments she was standing in front of a full-length mirror. The dress was not just on her; it *was* her. She felt years younger. She stood taller. Walked smarter. There was no doubt about it. She *had* to get the dress. Yes, cash was a little short, but no problem. In the blink of an eye and a flash of the plastic, the dress was hers.

That's when she walked through Kitchen Appliances

and saw *the* dishwasher. It was the very same high-end model she had been dreaming of for three months now. She had already shopped the consumer magazines—it was rated a best buy. Now it was being discontinued. The sign read SPECIAL DISCOUNT—SAVE $100! BUT ONLY THROUGH FRIDAY! It was actually good stewardship to buy it now, she reasoned to herself.

Yes, cash was a little short, but no problem. In the blink of an eye and a flash of the plastic, the dishwasher was *hers*.

That's when she walked by the pet store and saw *the* dog. For years the family had talked about getting a King Richard Special Edition Multicolored AKC Best Pure-Hearted Terri-Spaniel. And there in the window was one! Not just *any* one, *the* one. The cutest, most lovable ball of curly, multicolored fur that she had ever seen, with the most beautiful black eyes—windows into the purest of dog hearts—pleading with her for rescue, begging for refuge in her warm and loving home.

In a flash, the thought came to Eloise: *Muffin. Her name is Muffin.* How did she know that? And then in another flash, another thought came to her: *No one could love Muffin more than I do.* She had named the dog the moment their eyes met.

Suddenly, Eloise realized she wasn't alone. Standing next to her, looking in the window at *her* Muffin, was a middle-aged couple, both with shifty eyes. One of *those* couples, no doubt. What if Muffin went home with the shifty family? The thought hit her like a rolled-up newspaper, *They'll beat and mistreat her for the smallest stain on the carpet or even one ill-timed bark*. She couldn't let them harm her dog.

That's when she saw something she hadn't noticed before. Actually, it had been taped on the window for three weeks, through dozen of dogs, but it appeared out of nowhere for Eloise. A fluorescent orange sign that screamed: $200 OFF THIS WINDOW DOG! TODAY ONLY!

Two hundred dollars off! She almost fell backward. A new member of the family for two hundred dollars off! What were the odds?! This was amazing! This was *destiny*. It was an answer to prayer . . . even though she hadn't actually prayed about it. But, of course, Eloise smiled as she thought to herself, *That's God for you!* knowing her needs before she even had a chance to pray.

Yes, cash was a little short, but no problem. In the blink of an eye and a flash of the plastic, the dog was hers. Saved from the shifty couple and all set to go home.

But in reality, the dress, the dishwasher, and the dog were not hers. They were owned by the credit card company until Eloise paid for them. And if she paid just minimum payments, the dress, the dishwasher, and the dog would only cost her a few thousand more than if she had waited to pay cash. What a deal! *For the credit-card company.*

Through impulse buying, through the entrapment of *gotta get it now*, Eloise had just followed the same Skinny Rabbit Trail as her husband. A trail where she could triple her possessions in no time. But she didn't possess any of these things. They possessed *her*.

THE PERFECT-BODY TRAIL

Eloise stood at the Wal-Mart checkout stand, idly gazing at the magazine covers placed there to lure shoppers waiting in line. The photo of the trim and slim beauty in a bikini smiled her assurance that the headline above her was true: "I lost 50 pounds in five weeks. And so can you!" Eloise wasn't fat, really, but she had begun to notice that her dresses were getting harder to button, and squeezing into her old jeans now required writhing and gyrations that would do justice to MTV videos. She couldn't let herself go to pot like some of her classmates at their last reunion. She had to look like that magazine model. She snatched up the magazine and plopped it into her shopping cart.

Millions of people are chasing a skinny body without realizing it's another Skinny Rabbit. We see airbrushed models in magazines and makeup-plastered stars on television, and we get an image fixation. We believe we have to fit into a certain size or have guns for arms from pumping iron night and day. But there's a price to pay for linking your life to your body image. Like the woman who sat in my counseling office recently after too many face-lifts and body adjustments, furious that her grandchildren had dared to call her *Grandmother*. After all, she told me, "I'm not old!" Those kids could use her given name when they talked to her—but nothing with *grand* in it.

The fact is, despite all the medical touch-ups and tuck-ins available today (and this woman had almost all of them at least once), she wasn't getting younger—and neither are any of us who are above room temperature. If we are aging, that means we're breathing, and I for one choose breathing, along with all the wrinkles and age spots that come with it.

Certainly, I'm all for staying in great shape. I jog and try to eat healthily, except for major holidays and baseball games. But when your shape dictates your life, your emotions, your happiness, your marriage, your future, and whether or not you're old enough to have your grandchildren call you *Grandma* (when you are), you're on a Skinny Rabbit Trail. No, it's not fair that so many people today place so much stock in certain body types, looks, or labels. But you don't have to go down that trail.

You can't hold back the clock or the calendar, and as many aging movie stars and singers have painfully demonstrated (with excessive plastic surgeries and eyelids that are so tight, they look as if they can't blink!), age will eventually win out over tummy tucks and face-lifts. Muscles eventually yield to gravity no matter how much you try to pump or Botox them up. Exercise and staying in shape are important. But the pursuit of an ever-youthful body is chasing another Skinny Rabbit.

So far we've discussed only three of the five Skinny Rabbit Trails that the Smudleys followed: All Take and No Give, Possessive Possessions, and The Perfect Body. But don't go away. There are two more trails ahead.

4
TRAILS, TRAILS, AND MORE TRAILS

In this chapter we will examine two more common Rabbit Trails that cross the Smudleys' path. Each seems to offer so much yet leads us astray and leaves us with nothing.

THE PERFECTIONISM TRAIL

We've seen how possessions or even people can be Skinny Rabbits. But did you know that even *doing good* can turn into a Skinny Rabbit, tempting us down a dead-end trail? To see this happening, let's check in on Eloise and Elmer as they're about to follow another trail that will take them away from life, health, and even family and faith.

In spite of all her wonderful qualities—or maybe because of them—Eloise was a perfectionist. Although she didn't demand so much from others, she was extremely hard on herself. She justified her position with her life verse: "Whatever you do, work at it with all your heart, as working for the Lord, not for men" (Col. 3:23). Eloise was committed to excellence in everything. At first glance, that would seem like a good thing (Skinny Rabbits always look good at first), but watch what happened.

It was her perfectionism that drove Eloise to be the perfect wife, the perfect mother, the perfect volunteer in four groups, and the perfect alto with the perfect pitch in the church choir. Plus being the perfect daughter to care for her aging mother, plus being the perfect friend to help Alice deal with her family troubles, plus, plus, plus. The problem is, too many of these plusses can add up to a big negative. It's great to be committed to excellence. But when you fail to leave even a square inch of space in your life for flexibility or forgiveness or grace, you may end up getting committed. And I don't mean that in the good way.

The Bible says we're to have the mind of Christ. So here's the key question: Is perfectionism the path—the mind-set—God wants us to have?

Perfectionism puts us in a position of trying to do it all and to do it all in our own strength. Yet rarely is the all we have to give really enough. The opposite position to perfectionism is that of grace. Yes, we give life our absolute best, but we rely on God to fill in the gaps. For there will be gaps. And He's the one who gives us the strength we need to find rest, even when we're less than perfect. "My grace is sufficient for you," He promises (2 Cor. 12:9). Where we fall short, His grace fills in—it suffices.

Following God's paths will lead to life, rest, hope, and a real reward for real excellence. Following God breathes life into our own life and into the lives of others. Perfectionism stands on our air hose and refuses to lift its foot.

By trying to be excellent in everything and with everyone, Eloise was exceeding others' standards but never measuring up to her own. She longed to hear, "I've made it . . . I can sit down . . . I can rest." But those words never pulled up the chair. As energy, life, and even her faith drained away, life for Eloise became all duty. Deep inside she had come to the place where she didn't even like the friends she was performing for or her family for whom she was sacrificing. (The boys just *had* to have their T-shirts and underwear ironed, after all, even if they didn't appreciate her effort in doing it.) If the truth were known (gasp!), she had also grown weary of all the people depending on her to do so much, so well, at her church. In fact, while she hated to admit it, she liked them least of all.

Eloise wasn't alone in following the exhausting Skinny Rabbit Trail of perfectionism. Elmer had also headed down that trail but in a much different way. His garage was a mess, and his desk drawers a jumble, but there was one area that had to be just perfect for Elmer.

o o o

It always started with a Norman Rockwell picture in his mind—the kind of picture Elmer had missed out on as a child. Elmer's childhood family had been a shambles. There wasn't a single birthday or Christmas or vacation memory that Elmer wanted to remember. That's why his own family's *scrapbook of memories* was so important to him.

His children's memories would be different from his own . . . the family huddled together around a campfire by the tent, roasting marshmallows and sharing stories . . . the family fishing together on the lakeshore under a sprawling oak tree . . . the family gathered around the

Christmas tree as the snow fell softly outside the frosted-pane windows. He might have grown up with *Nightmare on Elm Street*, but it would be *It's a Wonderful Life* for his family. Their pictures would be perfect. He would see to it.

And then reality set in.

At the campout that Elmer had worked so hard to perfect, son Bobby—who had a weak stomach—ate too many marshmallows and threw up. On the fishing trip nobody caught any fish, but everybody got a sunburn. And at Christmas—the biggest family event of all—the toy train ran backward and caught on fire, the Christmas hamster died of a stroke, and Muffin the wonder dog ate all the Christmas cookies and threw up on Bobby, who got upset, and threw up again in return. Eloise and daughter Betsy cried. And Elmer yelled, "We're going to have a great Christmas memory if it kills us!"

He stood behind the camera and commanded, "Now smile as if your life depended on it!"

The problem with Elmer? He was making each of these cherished family times—these perfect, soft-focus photos in his mind—the big events designed to build perfect memories for his family and to make up for the terrible pictures of his own past. These special moments had to be perfect because he depended on them to define family relationships instead of focusing on the quality of day-to-day interaction. His mind-set of big-event perfectionism clouded his perspective. And what's more, the further down this trail he went, the less anyone in the family wanted to go with him. Or anywhere at all.

The fact is, life is lived in the everyday. It's in the rough and tumble of daily life where relationships are worked out, where we truly learn about becoming a family. Then vacations or fishing trips or Christmastime can be relaxing and truly become celebrations—celebrations of the growth that happens in the everyday.

Now let's go back to the main path and look at the Smudleys' next Rabbit Trail.

THE "WHEN I GET THAT . . ." TRAIL

Nine years ago:

Elmer couldn't wait. Another year on the assembly line and he'd be promoted to supervisor of Pickle Jar Labeling with higher pay and nicer perks.

Eight years ago:

Elmer couldn't wait. Another two years as supervisor of Pickle Jar Labeling and he'd be promoted to manager of Pickle Jar Research and Development with even higher pay and even nicer perks.

Six years ago:

Elmer couldn't wait. Another three years as manager of Pickle Jar Research and Development and he'd be promoted to vice president of Pickle Jar Design with even *higher* pay, and even *nicer* benefits.

Now:

Elmer couldn't wait . . . to go home. Yes, he had made it all the way to the top. Yes, he had tremendous influence. Yes, he was making pickles safer for America. But was this *it*? Was this all there was?

For several years Elmer had been chasing a Skinny Rabbit down the "When I get that . . ." Trail. *That* could be a promotion or position or grand award or exalted title. That's when everything will be better. That's when our dreams will come true. There's nothing wrong with promotions that lift us up higher or positions that allow us greater influence or awards that open doors or titles that open even more doors. But if *more* is our goal— more influence, more power, more money—then we have a very shallow goal, and we are chasing a very Skinny Rabbit. Even if the Rabbit Trail ends in an Academy Award on top of our chest of drawers.

Several years ago I received a call from an acquaintance in Hollywood. In the rush of words, I heard, "Emergency . . . A private plane is coming to get you . . . I can't tell you more until you get here . . . You've just got to come . . . It's life and death, and *I'm not kidding* . . ." I called Cindy, my precious, patient wife, and got clearance to jump on the plane and try and be of help (with the promise that I'd call as soon as I could and let her know "the rest of the story"). I raced home, threw some clothes in a suitcase, and headed off to a large private airport near our home.

I've only been in a private jet twice. This was the first time. Sitting in those plush leather seats, I had no idea exactly where I was going. We landed near beautiful downtown Burbank. Soon we were driving through some of the most exclusive neighborhoods in the world, filled with some of the most beautiful homes I'd ever seen. I remember the car finally stopping in front of huge, ornate gates where guards carefully checked my ID. Then the gates opened, and there was a long drive up to a front door that was easily three times the size of mine at home.

And then I remember walking up a winding, *Gone with the Wind* staircase and into a room that was almost empty. Just a bed, a few chairs scattered on either side of the room, and an extremely large chest of drawers. On top of that chest sat an Academy Award. A *real* Academy Award. The mother of all celebrity awards, just a few feet from me.

And just a few steps away was the recipient of this grandest of awards: Shattered. Hurting. Lonely. Drained.

Most amazing to me was how barren the room was. You'd think a room with an Academy Award would have been filled with energy, promise, creativity, and life. Just think of the explosion of opportunities winning such a reward would bring! Instead, this huge room was as vacant and cold as a tomb. I soon found out that the room was, in fact, the end of a very long Skinny Rabbit Trail. And there before me was someone in tremendous pain—emotionally, physically, and spiritually beyond exhaustion. A person with so much emptiness after so many Skinny Rabbit Trails that life simply didn't matter anymore. Not the guards at the gate, not the big house, not the maids inside the house, or even his thousands of admirers. None of it—and none of the people who had come with it—had brought the life this person longed for. And the day it all crashed down was the day *after* winning the Academy Award. That morning he woke up to find out that even the greatest of awards—just a few feet away and with his name on it—couldn't bring real life. For that person, one of the greatest of all rewards should have been shaped like a Skinny Rabbit, not a statuesque figure.

A good friend of his had been flown in as well, and we did our best to help this person during the two days we were there. I shared what you will learn later in Chapter 8—"Wise Hunters to the Rescue"—and, thankfully, it seemed to help. At least, this person was up and at 'em in a few days and, from what I could tell on the outside, has never looked back. However, I think I am the one who learned the most from that experience—spending two days just five feet from an Oscar. I actually got to hold the award while I was there. A tall, extremely heavy, gold-plated figurine that looks great on a chest of drawers—but makes a lousy god.

All kinds of people chase after prizes or positions, awards or titles. These are people who picture themselves finally standing on that award platform or sitting in a corner office with their name on the door, not knowing that they're on top of a laundry chute that can drop in an instant, sending them into a free fall all the way to the bottom.

Let's be clear. Gaining that promotion or that degree or that award is great, if it's *not* your life. But no honor or position or achievement will be enough to become the real life you seek.

Elmer may have been tempted down this Skinny Rabbit Trail of position and achievement, but certainly not Eloise. She was a stay-at-home mom, after all. But believe it or not, she was heading down the same "When I get that . . ." Trail. For her, it came by thinking thoughts such as:

When we finally get debt-free, then Elmer and I will be happy.

When we finally get a housekeeper, then I can finally get some rest.

When the kids are out of the house, then Elmer and I can have time for each other.

It's healthy to look forward in life. The problem is, if we keep putting all our happiness, our rest, and our time for each other out there in the future, we'll miss valuable opportunities to live life in the now. Jesus said, "I have come that they may have life, and have it to the full" (John 10:10). That means fullness of life today. Not someday.

THIS WAY TO A TRULY
A-MAZ-ING LIFE!

YOU'RE DONE FOR!

The Bible also says, "Command those who are rich in this present world not to be arrogant nor to put their hope in wealth, which is so uncertain, but to put their hope in God, who richly provides us with everything for our enjoyment" (1 Tim. 6:17). This life, this abundance from God, this enjoyment is not just financial. It's about a quality that encompasses all of life. And it's not just a life someday in heaven. It's about God's kingdom and His will *here on earth* as it is in heaven. To depend on some future achievement or condition is to chase a rabbit that is not only too skinny to be worth the effort; it may never be caught at all. After all, tomorrow never comes. If you want life, you must find it in the today.

THE INCREDIBLE SHRINKING PLACE

Elmer was getting paid fairly well as vice president of Paula's Pickles, and he enjoyed a position of power over the entire pickle jar operation. He'd been with the company for nine years and had a strong reputation for being a man of his word.

But something was nagging at him. He was still wrestling with the question, is this all there is? But more than that, he was also wrestling with his environment at work. The corporate culture at Paula's Pickles praised pickles, not people. In the boardroom he heard snide remarks and demeaning jokes from higher management who looked down on the assembly-line workers. These were considered the little pickle people—gherkins in the world of pickles.

For most of his career, Elmer had shielded his staff from this culture. But as he rose in the ranks, he was pressured to be more of a pickle person than a people person. This mentality carried through in corporate expectations.

At Paula's Pickles, work comes before family. This rule isn't in the employee manual or even written into the mission statement. It's in the office lights that burn late into the night, belonging to the managers who regularly put in sixty, sometimes seventy, hours a week.

Elmer's light now often burned evenings as well. He came home late at night, drained. He dreaded getting up in the morning. His spirit was withering. He was going through the motions of doing his job—and he did it well—but his heart wasn't in it.

Elmer also volunteered once a week at the Junior Business Clinic, a special mentoring class for inner-city youth. He coached young kids whom society had written off, and it was the highlight of his week. Last week he gave a little encouragement to an eleven-year-old boy and enjoyed seeing the young man's eyes light up. Elmer read a lot in those eyes: *Someone approves of me! Someone cares for me! Someone believes in me!* It caught his heart by surprise, and he had to turn away for a moment. Of everybody in the world, God had used him at that very moment to speak life into the next generation.

Elmer couldn't wait to get home and tell Eloise about it. As he shared what happened, Eloise saw something in her husband that she hadn't seen in a while—enthusiasm. It was a welcome change. She had been concerned for Elmer, watching him slowly wither at work. He had begun getting crabby about little things, and that wasn't like him. At that moment she saw the man she fell in love with years ago come to life again.

In getting caught up in the corporate culture, Elmer had followed a Skinny Rabbit to the Incredible Shrinking Place—a place that shrivels the soul by sucking out all the humanity and leaving only a mechanism capable of robotic function. He was clamped to that shrinking place by "golden handcuffs"—a situation that pays so well that one feels bound to it. Elmer began to realize that although he performed well in his job and the salary was hefty, this wasn't the place where he belonged. It didn't fit him. Elmer was a people person trapped in a pickle-praising environment with little regard for people.

A shrinking place is a bog where small thinking tries to keep you small too. It's a place that tries either to "cubicle-ize" you in a little gray box or chain you to a perpetual treadmill of busyness. You'll find shrinking places at work, even at church. Entire towns can be such shrinking places. (Nothing wrong with small towns, but there is something wrong with small thinking.)

Eloise, meanwhile, had also followed a Skinny Rabbit to a shrinking place. She, too, was mired in that bog, but she didn't realize it. After all, she was using her gifts full-time at their church. On Sunday nights she coordinated the Adoption Support Program to come alongside adoptive families with meals, baby-sitting, and other practical help. On Monday nights she was part of a counseling ministry team to help hurting people. Tuesday nights she led a class for young moms; Thursday nights was choir; and Saturday mornings she volunteered her time at a food-share project for the homeless.

Unlike her husband, Eloise was fully functioning in a place that recognized her gifts. But just like her husband, she was totally drained. She was caught up in *good* things instead of *God* things—the things that seemed right to do instead of the things that God had *called* her to do. As she took on more and more tasks without boundaries or help, her joy in helping others (not to mention her energy and health) dwindled. Church became a shrinking place for Eloise—a place with unlimited needs that drained and withered her. It may be hard to believe that getting caught up in church activities can be following a Skinny Rabbit, but it does happen. A lot.

Both Elmer and Eloise were on the verge of burnout. The Skinny Rabbit Trails they were following already had taxed them emotionally and spiritually. While it hadn't yet surfaced into hospitalization or an accident, it was also taxing them physically.

Studies show that stress and burnout affect your immune system and can cause migraines, digestive maladies, high blood pressure, skin problems, and heart disease. For some of these problems, the dead end is death—you become roadkill on the Skinny Rabbit Trail.

Skinny Rabbit Trails like the five we've just highlighted draw you off God's path and dump you in the wilderness of wilted hopes and bankrupt dreams. Don't kid yourself. The more steps you take down any of these trails, the more you'll find yourself isolated, lost, bogged down, and crushed.

So is that it? Only five trails? Just avoid all-take-and-no-give people and triple-your-possessions schemes; cross off the quest for a skinny body and perfectionism; keep from looking to future "When I get . . ." positions? Then will you be safe from the Incredible Shrinking Place? Are those the only Rabbit Trails to stay alert for?

TRAILS, TRAILS, AND MORE TRAILS

Not at all! Unfortunately, the five trails we have just identified are only a few in a forest full of them.

Do you suppose there's any chance you might be on one of those trails? Hmmm. Maybe we'd better pause and check that out.

5
ARE YOU ON
A RABBIT TRAIL?

Before we move on, let's talk for a moment about your story. Are you on a Skinny Rabbit Trail? Not sure? Well then, *are you even asking the question?* If not, you should be. Every day. You not only should be questioning the things that could beckon you down Rabbit Trails right now, you also should be teaching your kids to avoid Skinny Rabbits in their own lives—saving them years of heartache in the future.

Before we move on to talk about how to get off of Rabbit Trails and how to get out of the pits and bogs you find yourself in, I want you to pause and make this story up-close-and-personal. You may be starting to wonder whether or not you are currently chasing any Skinny Rabbits. You may be on a Rabbit Trail and not know it because it's one that I haven't specifically identified here. But I hope that by looking at the examples in the previous two chapters, you get the idea of what a Skinny Rabbit Trail can look like and use them to assess your own path.

In those chapters I listed only a few of the hundreds of Skinny Rabbit Trails that can blind your perspective, rob your future, and restrain your potential. The purpose of those examples was to give you the basic idea— to show how almost anything can lure you down a Rabbit Trail before you know it. Sometimes you're not even lured. You are working hard, trying to keep up, trying to meet all your deadlines and responsibilities, trying to do all you're supposed to do and do it well. Then suddenly you find you're no longer on the trail of the Great Stag. You've lost your bearings, and you have no idea where you went wrong. All you know is that where you are is not where you want to be.

So before we move on, spend a moment thinking about whether a Rabbit Trail may have pulled you aside from your quest. To start your thinking, here's an example from someone who read an article I wrote on Skinny Rabbits for our Web site at www.StrongFamilies.com:

> The Skinny Rabbit that I found myself chasing liter-
> ally my whole life was a relationship with my absen-
> tee father. I truly believed that if I had a relationship
> with my father—who apparently did not want a rela-
> tionship with me—all things in life would become
> plain and clear.

Well, my father stepped back into my life earlier this year. I've attempted to welcome him completely. However, it has not been easy. I simply do not trust that he's here to stay. Despite his sometimes overwhelming attempts to reassure my family and me that he has changed, I still find myself in a very protective mode. I am not as concerned about protecting myself as protecting my children. I do not want them to experience the same feeling of rejection that I have lived with my whole life.

His return—which I had prayed for most all my life—feels empty. I realized that I wanted to shoehorn him into the void that only God can fill. When he came back into my life, I realized he was a Skinny Rabbit. I had been on the wrong trail in my expectation that he would provide the substance to my life that I'd hoped for.

Realizing all this was a wake-up call. It helped me to stop wasting time focusing on my father and allowed me to realize that I should have been chasing my heavenly Father with the same fervency and zeal in search of the fulfillment of the void in my life.[1]

I can relate to that e-mail in a big way. It's an echo of my own story and a Skinny Rabbit Trail that I followed for too many years. Like Robert's father, my father also left when I was very young. I was only two months old. I never met my father until nearly twenty years after he'd left our home. But during those two decades when my father was gone, fully a thousand times I thought, *If I could just meet my dad, everything would be better.* But when I did meet him, much like Robert, I found that our relationship wasn't real and things didn't automatically get better. The time we spent together didn't explode with all the life and energy and hope and reversal of loss that I was so sure would happen.

After becoming a Christian I did my best to honor my father until the day he died. But for too many years I thought he held the key to life. That was time I spent with Robert on a Skinny Rabbit Trail.

HOW CAN I KNOW IF I'M ON A SKINNY RABBIT TRAIL?

Maybe you're not sure that you are chasing a Skinny Rabbit. Perhaps you're vaguely aware that something is out of kilter in your life, but you can't quite put your finger on what it is. So how can you tell whether you're on a Skinny Rabbit Trail?

No one who pursues a goal thinks it's unworthy. If we did, we wouldn't pursue it. So obviously when we chase rabbits, we're momentarily deceived into thinking we're onto something good. What we need are early clues to warn us that this is nothing but a Skinny Rabbit Trail.

I will give you a little exercise to assist you in recognizing clues that can alert you that you might be chasing a Skinny Rabbit and just how far down the trail you may be.

Feelings are not generally valid guides to real truth. As you know, feelings can deceive you if you depend on them for the wrong purpose. "If it feels good, it must be right" is one of the most dangerous things you can say. Your feelings often deceive you because they lure you to do things that promise glittering, immediate benefit, ignoring the cold, hard fact that there is a grim payoff at the end.

On the other hand, bad feelings—feelings of depression, tiredness, forgetfulness, disappointment, isolation, or irritability—can be like warning lights on the car dashboard, indicators that something is not right and needs immediate attention. Just as a flashing engine light or a knocking sound in a running car can tell you something is wrong inside the engine, those bad feelings listed above—especially if they persist—can be signs telling you that something is wrong inside your life. They may be strong indications that you are on a Skinny Rabbit Trail.

The short exercise that follows can help you use your feelings to determine whether you are on a Skinny Rabbit Trail and how far down it you may have traveled.

SKINNY RABBIT TRAIL TRACKER

Read the following statements and put a check mark in the box beside each one that has applied to you in the past three months. Then tally up the results at the end. Whatever your score, remember that it's not where you are today that counts but it's where you can be when you get your life back on the trail of the Great Stag. So be honest, and know there's real help in the pages to come.

❑ 1. I get tired easily.

❑ 2. I get upset when others tell me, "You don't look so good lately."

❑ 3. I feel that my prayers are getting no further than the ceiling.

❑ 4. I feel that God has abandoned me.

❑ 5. I sometimes find myself crying for no discernible reason.

❑ 6. I feel discouraged and disappointed in the world around me.

❑ 7. I've been getting more forgetful.

❑ 8. I seem to be doing more but enjoying less.

❑ 9. I find myself saying (again and again), "Oh, he'll change" or "Oh, she'll change."

❑ 10. I feel that I've lost my sense of purpose.

❏ 11. I have periods of extreme doubt that life is
worth the effort.

❏ 12. I have trouble feeling happy.

❏ 13. I'm not able to laugh at a joke about myself.

❏ 14. Sex seems to be more trouble than it's worth.

❏ 15. I have very little to say to people.

❏ 16. I feel lonely most of the time.

Scoring: If the number of boxes you checked are:

0–3   Congratulations! Looks like you're not on a
Skinny Rabbit Trail at all. (But keep reading
to make sure you stay away from them.)

4–6   You've taken a few steps down a Skinny Rabbit
Trail. You're not headed toward a major
disaster yet, but read on to see which Skinny
Rabbit may be luring you to ruin.

7–9   Sure enough—you're on the trail of a Skinny
Rabbit.

10–12 Red Alert! You're not only on a Skinny Rabbit
Trail—you may have stepped into a bog.

13–16 A Skinny Rabbit has gotten you so far off
course, you've lost all scent of the Great Stag
and how to find your way back to its trail.

Don't be prideful if you got a low score, thinking
you're above such obvious distractions. And don't despair

if your score reaches into the stratosphere. Stay with me, and I'll show you how you can get off that Rabbit Trail and back on the tracks of the Great Stag.

Think of this exercise as preliminary. It is designed to help you begin assessing your own situation. At this point you're not necessarily trying to identify or determine your Skinny Rabbit, but merely to realize that you may be on the trail of one. After you've learned more about Skinny Rabbits, their trails, and the hazards of following them, I'll give you a more advanced and detailed way of getting down to the real nitty-gritty of identifying the actual Skinny Rabbits that may be wrecking your life.

6
BOGS, PITS, SWAMPS, AND CAVES

Skinny Rabbit Trails not only draw you away from a path of purpose but also tend to lead you to dead ends that bog you down and keep you from getting back on course. In fact, this is one important way that you can spot a Skinny Rabbit Trail. While you're trying your best, you're really not moving along the path . . . just standing still, spinning wheels, treading water, lost to all that's meaningful; going through the motions but feeling no joy, no sense of purpose or gratification or accomplishment. Being bogged down by following a Skinny Rabbit Trail too far is almost a guarantee that you will start to die emotionally, spiritually, and sometimes even physically.

This describes the bogs, swamps, pits, and caves we fall into when we get lost chasing the Skinny Rabbit. Let's look at some of these hazards more closely.

THE BOG OF PRIDE

You figure that you're doing all right. Better than that, you're doing *great*. It's taken a while, and you've worked hard to get where you are, but now you're pretty much *there*. To prove your unselfishness, you'd like to train others to achieve the kind of success you've achieved. Thank God you don't have a problem with pride! In fact, you're thinking you could probably skip this section altogether. But maybe it would be good to read it anyway, just in case you ever get the opportunity to help someone else with his or her pride problem.

rabbitus skinnius, v. To think only of and too much of yourself. See *pride*.

Pride is like a pair of designer sunglasses. They make you think you look cool, but they cloud your vision to where you can't see the light of truth. Imagine one of our mighty hunters in pursuit of the Great Stag, wearing a set of these dark glasses. He thinks he looks suave and sophisticated to the other hunters, but what is not readily apparent—until it's too late—is that he can't see clearly enough to follow the track of the Great Stag.

In fact, pride eventually blinds you. With pride, you're so focused on yourself that you can't see where you're going. And since you're blind to any faults you may have ("Faults? What faults?"), you're vulnerable to tripping up. That's why pride comes before a fall.

Where pride blinds, humility opens up your eyes to see the truth.

"For whoever exalts himself will be humbled, and whoever humbles himself will be exalted" (Matt. 23:12). You have a choice. You can humble yourself or you can be humbled. You can recognize your pride and come down off of it, or you can fall flat. Be assured, you'll eventually come down, one way or the other. If it's pride that pushes you on your quest toward your goal, then don't wear those sunglasses! Have the humility to take them off. Then once you can see clearly again, look around to see if you've gotten off the trail of your quarry and wandered down a Rabbit Trail. If you find that's what you've done, then turn around (what the Bible calls *repent*). Moving away from death starts with taking steady steps back toward truth and life. And you can't do this wearing the sunshades of pride.

The problem is that prideful people don't like the idea of backtracking (any more than they can stomach the idea of apologizing to anyone they may have hurt). But prideful people also hopelessly stay on the trail of a Skinny Rabbit, never realizing they're not still following the Great Stag. Never seeing their need until it's too late and they are mired up to their sun-shaded eyeballs in a deadly bog.

THE BOG OF FALSE HUMILITY

On the flip side of pride is false humility—thinking lower of yourself than God intended. Humility is desirable, but self-flagellation is not. Humility is admirable; wimpiness is not. Humility is commendable, but self-condemnation is not. False humility will keep you thinking small and living small. "What am I doing with these mighty hunters on the trail of the Great Stag?" whispers false humility. "Why should I think I can achieve anything grand like this? I'm not a great hunter. I'm not even a very good hunter. In fact, I have trouble killing a fly with a swatter. I don't deserve even to be in this hunt."

If you travel with your head hanging like this, you'll lose track of your quarry and wind up in a bog. And once you land there, you're likely to remain hopelessly stuck, because you'll use your false humility as an excuse to wallow in hopelessness, never getting back to the path of your worthwhile dreams and goals.

False humility is actually a backhanded kind of pride because, like pride, it does not look outside the self. Pride says, "I have it in myself to do it all." False humility says, "I don't have it in myself to cut melted butter." But notice that the thing in common with both attitudes is the insistence on looking only to the self.

The key to avoiding—or getting unstuck from—the bog of false humility is to look outside yourself for the strength you need to accomplish worthwhile dreams and goals. The apostle Paul gives us the source of that strength: "I can do everything through him who gives me strength" (Phil. 4:13). True humility isn't about being a doormat. It's about knowing where your strength comes from—from God, not from yourself.

THE CAVE OF FEAR

Fear is a lie. Fear keeps you cowering in a cave, afraid to join in the pursuit for dread of failure, harm, ridicule, or some other imagined bogey lurking out there in the forest. Fear says, "Stay inside, stay safe," when faith says, "Go! Get on the trail of your Great Stag."

The only healthy fear is the fear of the Lord, which

is the gateway to wisdom. All other fears—including the fear of failing, fear of the future, fear of what others think—are all part of a debilitating lie that keeps you hunkered down in the back corner of your cave while other hunters take the risk, follow God as their leader, and go for the prize.

"Fear of man will prove to be a snare, but whoever trusts in the LORD is kept safe" (Prov. 29:25).

THE SWAMP OF BUSYNESS

Any of us can get lost in the swamp of busyness. In fact, it happened to our old friend, Elmer Smudley. You remember Elmer. He wanted to rise as far as he could up the corporate ladder of Paula's Pickle Factory. He stretched upward with everything he had to reach that next rung—and it was worth every bit of the effort. After all, this was the ladder of success. And finally he made it! He worked hard; he kept at it; he kept focusing on that next rung, that next stretch. And then . . . breakthrough! Another rung! Another climb!

He climbed several rungs in a row, now really gaining momentum! More money, more power, more prestige. But also more deadlines, more stress, more time away from Eloise and his family. Then one day he stepped back and realized he was not climbing the rungs of a ladder at all; he was climbing the rungs of a hamster wheel!

He was caught on the hamster wheel of busyness. Up close it looks a lot like a ladder. It appears that you are climbing fast. Moving up. But you're really not going anywhere. You're running in a circle.

Often a husband will be running hard on his hamster wheel while his wife is running just as hard on her own hamster wheel. It appears that they're doing life together. It appears that they're going somewhere together. Well, sure! They're in the same cage. But it's a cage all the same. And the only place they're going together is nowhere.

You'll find hamster wheels of busyness not only at work but also at school, at church, in volunteer and civic organizations—they're everywhere. Please understand, there's nothing wrong with hard work. In fact, Proverbs —a book penned by the wisest king who ever lived— praises diligence. "All hard work brings a profit, but mere talk leads only to poverty" (Prov. 14:23).

The problem comes when you're so entrapped by busyness that you don't have time for the truly important things—things more significant and rewarding but usually less urgent. Your devotional time with God rarely seems urgent; neither is a date night with your spouse or play and talk time with your kids. But the urgent things scream for your attention *now*! That's when the important but quieter priorities are frequently shoved aside.

It's a good thing to step off the wheel and ask yourself, *Where am I really going? Am I missing out on the important things? Is everything I'm doing worth it, or am I chasing a Skinny Rabbit? Is there a way to incorporate the important things into my busy lifestyle?*

That last question is actually a trick question for busy people. When you're too busy, you're trying to fit too much into a finite schedule. The secret to incorporating the important things is not to find some technique for fitting even more in but rather to let go of the busy things that matter less. Weed out the *urgent* and keep the *important*.

If you have trouble discerning the urgent from the important, take the 10/100 test. Ask yourself, will this matter ten years from now? Will this matter one hundred years from now? This test will help you tell the difference between the Skinny Rabbit Trails and the trail of the Great Stag.

THE CAVE OF FANTASY

You're headed down the trail in pursuit of the Great Stag. You've been on the trail for a long time. You're tired. You're hungry. Sometimes the whole quest just seems too hard, too tedious, too filled with difficulties. Then suddenly you spot something very strange. It's a beautiful door, set in the side of a cliff covered with vines and flowers. Weird.

You're intrigued, and you wonder where it leads. You imagine Aladdin's cave of wonders, filled with bright, glittering treasures. Maybe it's a place where you can rest from the trail for a moment. Maybe it's a diversion that can renew your enthusiasm. Maybe it's a place where you can temporarily escape all the hardships of the trail. So you cautiously step through the door . . . and find yourself in another world, a magical place where you can actually walk through your thoughts and watch your dreams played out on stage as if they were real.

God gave each of us an imagination—a playground in our minds on which to consider ideas. But this wonderful place can trap you. You can tell you're in danger of being trapped in that cave when you find yourself spending more time in your imagination than in the real world. You like it there because in your imagination everything is perfect. You can have excitement with no risk, possessions at no cost, power with no responsibility, pleasure with no consequences. So once you've gone through that door, why go back when there's so much to see and do and experience here in this alternate world?

Here's the danger: After spending time in that glittering but artificial world, you hear the door to reality close behind you. You hear a lock engage. And the scariest part of all is that *you don't care.*

The door to that cave can be the lure of your computer screen. I'm not about to tell you that all computer games are evil. But when you find yourself spending hours and hours playing each day, something has shifted. You can be sure you're spending way too much time behind the door marked Fantasy when you hear friends and family say things such as:

- "Where have you been? I haven't seen you in forever!"
- "We really need to talk, but you've been preoccupied."
- "When was the last time we got together?"
- "Dad, can we talk sometime? We haven't done that in a *long* time."

- "Please take me to the playground—when can we go?"

If you're hearing these kinds of comments, don't just write them off. Your family and friends are trying to tell you something—something important.

"Andy" was an expert in *World of Warcraft*, a role-playing game engaging more than six million people online around the world, all of them playing at the same time. He became a guild leader—a highly coveted position that only a select few manage to achieve.

To keep up with the exciting challenges of the game and his responsibility to guild members, Andy put in around thirty hours a week. He started to withdraw from other things he enjoyed—like playing guitar and writing. He gained about thirty pounds. He no longer had time for his friends. And then he lost his girlfriend, someone he genuinely loved. In going through the fantasy door, he had chased a Skinny Rabbit and lost what was genuinely important.

Andy was at the top of his game but at the bottom of his life. He had given up all his close friends and girlfriend—for what? To gain treasures in pixilated images? Pride had kept him from saying it for too long, but it was true. Fantasy had become more "real" than real, more to be desired than real life. At least for a while. At least until his girlfriend left, and he finally realized how alone he was, even in the midst of six million online "friends." He forgot about what was real, and his life dried up as a result.

As Andy tells us, "From my vantage point as a guild decision maker, I've seen [fantasy games] destroy more families and friendships and take a huge toll on individuals than any drug on the market today, and that means a lot coming from an ex-club DJ." After a year of pouring his heart and soul into the game, he told the guild he was leaving. They hardly noticed. "Three days later, I didn't exist anymore."[1]

The gaming fantasy leads us down a Skinny Rabbit Trail by laying before us a promising banquet. A long table full of the most delectable, mouthwatering, succulent Turkish Delight (remember Narnia?) you could imagine. But none of it is *real*. It's an imaginary meal that brings no real nourishment for our lives or life to our souls. If you or your kids struggle in the gaming area, I highly recommend that you read *Playstation Nation* by Olivia and Kurt Bruner. It's an outstanding book by one of our faculty members at The Center for Strong Families. It will open your eyes.

For many this fantasy door leads to an even more sinister place. In this day and age, it's hard not to know of or to have been affected by someone in our circle of friends or family who hasn't gone through a fantasy door marked Pornography.

Don't believe the lie that says you're strong enough

to handle it. It's powerfully attractive—as any fantasy door is. But it's a cheap thrill that's actually very costly—sucking the very life out of you and trapping you in a cave that is hard to get out of. This cave darkens your conscience, drives a wedge of duplicity into your being, and contaminates your marriage bed.

That fantasy door may look to be a tempting respite from the grind of the trail, but if you expect to be successful on your quest, you must avoid it. You could easily enter that cave and never emerge again. As Mark Twain said, "It's easier to stay out than to get out."

THE PIT OF ISOLATION

Remember. Skinny Rabbit Trails move you farther and farther from anything that brings you life and purpose. The bogs, caves, and pits along these trails can trap you and keep you from ever finding your way back. One of the most insidious of those hazards is the pit of isolation.

It starts by being so busy that you have to cut out time with friends. Even a short time to work out or have coffee or attend church or a game together. Your e-mail in-box bulges, and you don't care. Your phone rings unanswered. Church becomes optional. Even family gatherings become, at best, a chore. That's the first step.

Then an entire philosophy grows to justify the isolation. One of its tenets, for example, is: "Hey, I can just have church by myself—just me and God." Whether it's busyness or depression or shame or deliberate choice or all the above, you find it harder to have quality time with real friends. You become so intense in your pursuit of your Skinny Rabbit that you wrap yourself up in yourself, and all relationships become peripheral.

This pit of isolation is one of the scariest perils lurking on the trail of the Skinny Rabbit. Why? Look up the word *isolation* in Greek. It's the word *thanatos*. And its translation? *Death*. Isolation is death. The more you isolate yourself, the more you die inside. No matter what Rabbit Trail you pursue, you are vulnerable to falling into this pit of isolation that can result in death. I don't mean death in the sense that you'll keel over and someone will call the undertaker. I'm talking about isolation from real life, from nourishing relationships with real meaning.

For example, pornography, the fantasy hazard I've just warned against, is one of the most insidious isolators— and thus pits of death—that you can encounter. Every step you take toward illicit fantasy and what isn't real is a step away from life . . . killing off real relationships and opportunities to grow or to help others. Pornography moves us away from real people—from our loved ones, even from God. Because of the shameful acts and images involved in pornography, it pushes us away from a real *life*style and lures us to embrace a death-style.

Fall into the pit of isolation, and you're cut off from

any taste of living water that could sustain you. That living water flows through relationships—your relationship with others and your relationship with Jesus, the "realest" of people.

Many trails can lead to the pit of isolation. Most of us remember a guy and girl back in high school who were so wildly in love with each other that they spent every moment together to the exclusion of all friends. Their neglected friends gradually drifted away. Eventually, when the couple broke up, they found themselves completely isolated, without any friends at all. What a sad place to be! But it's a typical place for far too many when they wake up alone.

And what a dangerous place to be. I know of a well-loved pastor who was amazingly blessed with discernment —the keen wisdom to see into a situation and know intuitively what to do. This pastor had a winning personality and the ability to communicate well to his congregation and to the media. His church and his influence multiplied. It seemed everything he touched was blessed.

But as he became more and more busy, he became more and more isolated from friends who could hold him accountable. And without accountability he drifted into a private sin, causing a secret shame to grow inside him like an ominous shadow over his heart. One day his sin came to light for all to see. He lost his church. His influence. His reputation.

It took him twenty years to rise to the top . . . and just three days to fall to the bottom.

You know people like that as well. And don't think it couldn't be you. It could happen to any of us. Proverbs says, "He who separates himself seeks his own desire, he quarrels against all sound wisdom" (18:1 NASB). We need friends. We need interaction with others. "As iron sharpens iron, so one man sharpens another" (Prov. 27:17). Also, "Faithful are the wounds of a friend, but deceitful are the kisses of an enemy" (Prov. 27:6 NASB).

The more you hang around quality friends—friends willing to support you and confront you in love when you need it—the sharper and safer you'll be. Real friends are like guardrails: they'll do everything they can to help you stay on the path of purpose and life. If only that fallen pastor had had even one real friend, his life might have been different.

But when you isolate yourself from friends—when you don't have those guardrails—it's easy to drift off the highway. The consequences can range from a rough ride on the shoulder to a plunge off the cliff.

THE TAR PIT OF LITTLE WHITE LIES

It starts as a little sin. You try to cover up for something by telling a little lie. And it gets a bit worse. Now you try to cover the sin *and* the little lie by a slightly larger dishonesty. You try to ignore the whole mess and put it behind you, but it comes back again. More lies. Bigger lies. The problem gets deeper. Messier.

You have just fallen into the tar pit of little white lies. The more you fight to get out of this tar pit, the more stuck you become. The more you try to hide sin with lies, the stickier the situation gets.

Chasing Rabbit Trails makes us vulnerable to this tar pit. Usually when we take the quick, easy route and go after less than the best, we're not too proud of it. We don't want others to know what we are up to. The easy way to hide these pursuits? Lie about them. Make up a story. Then suddenly we're in that pit that requires stories to cover the stories to cover the stories, and soon we're stuck in a muck of lies.

The only way to get clean . . . is to come clean. Face the embarrassment of exposing the lie, confess the cover-up, be honest about our dishonesty, allow healing to begin, and repent of ever doing such a thing again.

THE PIT OF DEPRESSION

You lie in your bed, staring at the ceiling, thoughts swirling like fog in your brain. A heavy shadow weighs almost palpably on your chest—a darkness that refuses to lift. You try to think bright, positive thoughts, but they're all smothered by the engulfing darkness that seems closer and more real.

You've chased the Skinny Rabbit and fallen into the pit of depression. It's a deep, dark place where grievous ponderings echo in the emptiness of your heart. And the only hope is a tiny circle of light up above—a light that seems to be fading.

Chasing Skinny Rabbits *can* lead to depression for several reasons. Maybe you've spent time pursuing the wrong thing, and you've come up empty or with a prize not worth the effort—all the while you've been diverted from the path to more rewarding goals. Or you're still chasing the rabbit and dog-tired from the endless trails that seem to have stolen from you any sense of purpose. These are significant losses, and when the reality of them hits, it can easily lead to depression. It steals years from your life that can never be recovered.

A good definition of *depression* is anger turned inward. You are angry over these losses—angry with your own culpability in causing them and frustrated with the impossibility of undoing the past. Or maybe you're angry at a person who led, pushed, or deceived you into following a Rabbit Trail. Or maybe you're angry with God for letting bad things happen to you when you were trying so hard. All of your anger is eating away your life and hope.

Of course, other things can cause depression as well, such as the loss of a loved one or even a chemical imbalance. Whatever the reason, most all of us will wrestle with depression at some time or another as we deal with anger, loss, or grief. It's a dark and terrible pit, and one that can take you down—permanently. If your symptoms persist or if you think about harming yourself or someone else, seek help immediately from your doctor or other qualified mental health professional.

However, since this book is about the effects of chasing down Skinny Rabbits, we will focus on depression resulting from pursuing unworthy goals and coming up empty-handed. Actually, any of the Rabbit Trails we've discussed in this book can result in depression. In fact, I would say that depression could result more often than not. Since depression is so common and so debilitating, we're going to take a little more space in dealing with it than we have the other pits, bogs, and caves we've mentioned. But while what I offer in the rest of this chapter is centered on depression, its application is much broader. These principles can actually help you avoid or get out of any of the hazards of chasing Skinny Rabbits.

Here's a Scripture passage that gives us the key to getting out of the pit of depression: *Godly sorrow brings repentance that leads to salvation and leaves no regret, but worldly sorrow brings death* (2 Cor. 7:10).

Notice that this verse mentions two kinds of sorrow. *Worldly* sorrow brings death, Paul tells us. That's depression. Sorrow without hope. Sorrow over losses and ruin that can't be changed. On the other hand, he tells us that *godly* sorrow brings repentance and leads to salvation. Instead of being sorrowful over what's already happened and can't be changed, be sorrowful for what you've done, and resolve to turn away from it and do it no more. That's the difference. When you turn away from your errors and sins and give them to the Lord with a commitment to place yourself in His hands, He pulls you from the pit and sets you back on the correct path.

That is the first step. The second is to look for that ladder of escape. God always provides a way of escape. If you find yourself trapped in the pit of depression, follow these steps to find that ladder.

1. Find someone to pull you out.

It's very hard to pull yourself out of the pit of depression. It's just like being in a physical pit; you need someone else to pull you out—whether it's a recommended therapist, a friend, a family member, a family doctor, a pastor, or a mentor. Find this person and make a commitment to meet with him or her regularly until you're out of the pit.

Remember the wisdom of Solomon, who said, "The heart of the discerning acquires knowledge; the ears of the wise seek it out" (Prov. 18:15). Don't think you can just spontaneously spring up from the pit of depression. It takes help and the hope that others can bring you—if

you are willing to seek and acquire it. Of course, that
means that you must . . .

2. Do something.

Improvement won't happen if you just sit and wait for
it to come. The word *life* in Greek means *movement*.
Move toward a goal. Physical exercise is often helpful.
Calling a friend is doing something. Visiting the family
doctor is doing something. Going for a walk around the
block with the dogs every night is doing something.
Whatever it is, *do something*. Another thing to do is . . .

3. Forgive.

If depression is anger turned inward, then you have
some forgiving to do. Forgiveness dissolves anger. It's a
vital step toward healing. Forgive the person who has
wronged you. (When you forgive him, you're saying you
no longer hold anything against him.) Forgive God. And
it's also important that you forgive yourself. I've found
one thing that always pushes us toward forgiveness of
our self and others, and that is . . .

4. Read the Psalms.

David, the author of most of the psalms, is a guy who
wrote from the heart and gut. It's real; it's raw. David is
brutally honest—sometimes mad at God, sometimes
frustrated at his circumstances, and sometimes down on

himself. Not every psalm has a happy "Ah-men" ending. But even in pouring out his laments, David looks to God for help:

> Why are you downcast, O my soul? Why
> so disturbed within me? Put your hope in God,
> for I will yet praise him, my Savior and my God.
> —Psalm 42:5–6

In the middle of his mess, David praises God—a perspective echoed by the prophet Isaiah, who talked about putting on "a garment of praise instead of a spirit of despair" (Isa. 61:3). David tells us in no uncertain terms that God is the answer to depression: *He lifted me out of the slimy pit, out of the mud and mire; he set my feet on a rock and gave me a firm place to stand* (Ps. 40:2).

As you read through Psalms, you'll discover how David chronicles a legacy of God's faithfulness in the middle of battle, betrayal, depression, and despair—the same kinds of obstacles we face today.

5. Be grateful.

Take a moment and write down three blessings—three things that went well today and why you're grateful for them. Do this for a week. Then think of three people who have touched your life in a positive way—a grandparent, a teacher, a friend, or someone else. Write each of them a letter expressing your thanks. Then deliver the letters, reading each one to the person yourself.

According to noted University of Pennsylvania psychologist Martin Seligman, an uncontrolled study revealed that 94 percent of severely depressed people who focused on being grateful ended up happier and less depressed. The people who continued to do these acts were measurably happier and less depressed as much as three to six months later.[2]

6. Get your eyes off yourself.

Start focusing on genuinely helping others—especially those in worse shape than you. It's healthy and helpful, both to them and to you.

A mother I met told me she had a seventeen-year-old son who had worked late at a fast-food place one night. He was walking home when someone shot and killed him at random. The best the police could come up with was to surmise it was some sort of dare from a gang.

The mom went through deep grief, anger, and depression for years. Then she finally realized that she had fallen into a pit and was merely wallowing in it. So with tears and a prayer, she got up, chose life, and got moving. Eventually she founded a mothers' group specifically geared to helping moms whose kids have been murdered. This act fulfilled something in her. Her group has helped hundreds of grieving moms across the country.

It's a great example of how one mom moved from isolation to helping others and how this act brought healing not only to her but also to others.

It's tough to be lured off course by a Skinny Rabbit. It's embarrassing to fall into pits, bogs, or swamps, or to hole up in caves. It's especially tough when we find ourselves despairing in the pit of depression. But there's something even worse . . . waking up one day to discover you have *become* that Skinny Rabbit for someone you care about—even yourself!

We'll talk about that in the next chapter.

7
THE SKINNY
RABBIT BRIDE

There have been some terribly infamous brides in his-tory. Frankenstein's Bride. The Runaway Bride. The Evil Bride that almost married the father of the twins in *The Parent Trap*.

And now, the Skinny Rabbit Bride.

It's obvious from the picture that no groom would willingly marry the Skinny Rabbit Bride. There is something dreadfully wrong with her. Skinny Rabbits lead people astray, getting them off the path of goodness, peace, and growth and leading them down a trail fraught with dangers, ending in disaster.

But did you realize that you could be a Skinny Rabbit yourself? Yes, *you*! Not only are Skinny Rabbits critters to avoid chasing; they are critters to avoid *becoming*.

ARE YOU FOR REAL?

Have you ever read *The Velveteen Rabbit*? I read this wonderful children's book to each of my daughters on the very first day of their lives. Sitting next to Cindy's hospital bed, with her holding our precious newborn, I read them their very first story about a frumpy, nondescript stuffed rabbit that became a little boy's best friend. (They couldn't understand a word, of course, but for Cindy and me it was a precious time.)

In the story, the little boy carried the pretend rabbit everywhere. Over the years he hugged most of its fur off. He even loved off one of its button eyes. But the Velveteen Rabbit didn't mind a bit what he looked like. He was just glad to have the boy's love. Like all Velveteen Rabbits, it was enough for him just to be there for the boy when he was cold, or lonely, or sick, or anytime. And to *be still*, even when the other toys with more bells and whistles made noise. In the end, this pretend bunny was loved so much, it actually became real.

With Skinny Rabbit Brides, it's just the opposite. They don't give love or invest themselves in any way. They just take and take. And in the process, they become less and less real.

Do you know anyone like that?

How does one become a Skinny Rabbit Bride? The easiest way to become someone else's Skinny Rabbit is to fail to keep our spiritual health robust. We focus on our own needs, our own wants, and ignore the needs of others. We become Skinny Rabbits when we use others to gratify our own needs or appetites, leaving them trapped in pits while we go on our merry, uncaring way. It can happen before you know it when your focus gets out of whack.

In fact, this is what happened to Becky, the girl who almost became the Skinny Rabbit Bride.

In just about every way we've described in this book, Becky was a Skinny Rabbit. Only you never would have known it by looking at her, or by her enormous popularity in high school and college. On the surface, she didn't look anything like the picture at the opening of this chapter. *On the surface*. A fairly shy, fairly normal kid in grade school, Becky hit puberty and exploded into a stunningly beautiful young woman. She looked like a twenty-year-old supermodel when she was thirteen. By seventeen she had a drawer full of business cards from photographers and agents—most of whom were real— who just walked up to her and wanted to put her on a magazine cover or in a film. By age twenty her looks had actually stopped traffic around the college she attended.

Once her beauty kicked in, it took Becky all of about thirty minutes to figure out how to use the assets God had given her to get almost anything she wanted. Friends. Dates. Prom invites. Gifts. A sparkling lineup of crowns from homecoming dances and beauty pageants. But what Becky liked most wasn't tiaras or the wake of girl-friends that always followed her like pilot fish feeding on leftovers from the shark. It wasn't even the second looks and gaping stares from men of all ages she'd long since taken for granted. Becky specialized in picking out a young man who was dating someone else, and then moving in and taking him away . . . just because she could. It's what made her a Skinny Rabbit.

The first time it happened, Becky wasn't even try-ing. It happened in middle school, just when she was beginning to blossom. A really cute, superpopular boy was dating another girl. But he fell hard for Becky. And all she did was sit next to him in algebra class—and watched as this boy twisted like an itchy earthworm to please her. He even wormed his way out of the relation-ship he was in just so he could date her. And as Becky watched his former girlfriend struggle with a broken heart after their relationship was over, somehow it made Becky feel incredibly powerful. *She* had done that. *She* was able to change the direction of people's lives just because of how she looked. To be able to cause so much turmoil in people's lives gave Becky a huge rush, stronger than a vente latte with six added shots. That kind of power was addicting.

Becky soon discovered something else: how quickly she tired of the boy who had given up everything to grovel at her feet. But that was a good thing; it meant she could easily jettison that relationship and go on to another one. More "extra shots." Another power trip. Of course, there *was* all that emotional collateral damage she left in her wake, but that certainly wasn't *her* fault. As the shattered relationships piled up, she remained blissfully immune to the pain and anger of her victims and their friends.

Becky honed her Skinny Rabbit skills to perfection at a large college in the South. She became a master manipulator, a skilled actress—skilled at moving people's emotions not on the big screen but in real life. When she sidled up to her chosen victim and blinked those beautiful eyes in surprise, it looked so innocent . . . so *real.* Each was an Emmy-quality performance, and she didn't have to put up with the paparazzi.

After Becky arrived at college, she quickly saw how important the whole religion thing was with her Southern sorority sisters. So, like a chameleon, she added that color to her palette. She actually prayed with some of the brokenhearted girls whose former boyfriends had *chosen* her over them. She found prayer a great way to deflect the damage she'd done. "It must be Your will, God," she'd pray, closing the discussion and allowing her to emerge unscathed. The duplicity of those feigned prayers didn't concern her. Hey, they got her what she wanted, didn't they? If God didn't like it, He had never told her. (Of course, she'd never asked God or listened for His voice, but for Becky that was beside the point.)

Becky had become the worst kind of Skinny Rabbit. She could turn off the air hose on someone's relationship without them ever knowing it was her hand that had twisted the valve shut. But even winning all the time can become boring, and that's why Becky decided one day to go for the Big Con—a long shot, even for her. Becky turned the full force of her charm on a dreamboat of a young man engaged to be married to someone else. Becky had taken out all kinds of relationships over the years, several of which might have gone on to become great marriages. But she had never actually taken the *ring* off a rival's finger and put it on her own.

That was Becky's new goal, and it was a tough one. It took her nearly a year, not to mention a summer internship, to get anywhere with this young man. (Surprise, surprise! Just happening to show up at the *very* company where he was doing his summer internship! What were the chances?) For a while the young man seemed immune to Becky's wiles, and it appeared that she had bitten off more than she could chew.

But on Thanksgiving of her senior year, the scales finally began to shift. He walked Becky to her car, and as the snow fell on her blonde hair and coat (white and lined with fake rabbit fur), he looked deeply into those fathoms-deep blue eyes. And she knew. As they stood in the parking lot, she could actually tell in his eyes the moment it happened. She'd seen it often enough.

A few hours later, he broke up with his fiancée. By Christmas, he had a new fiancée. Becky had won! It was like a Hallmark Channel movie, only *real*. She'd gotten the ring off the shattered girl's finger, and now it was sparkling on her own.

The two of them talked of a July wedding, but Becky knew their love wouldn't last until summer. She was already thinking of some way to keep the ring after they broke up.

Becky had achieved her goal.

Then the call came.

CALL OF THE GREAT STAG

It was Christmas vacation, and Becky had the entire month off. On the other end of the line was Kay, a new transfer student in Becky's sorority. She didn't know Kay well since she wasn't gorgeous enough to be a real rival; Kay was one of the *religious* ones, semipretty and nice enough to be seen with.

Kay had seen Becky praying with one of her victims, and it made her think Becky was a real believer. Kay told Becky that three girl counselors were down with the flu. Could Becky please, *please* come on supershort notice and be a room counselor for a Young Life ski trip?

It just so happened that Becky's fiancé was off with his family visiting his grandparents, and she was bored. This sounded perfect—a free ski trip at a first-rate resort! Becky was a serious skier, and more importantly, she looked great in a ski outfit. She could easily ditch the six girls in her cabin once they hit the slopes. She could do her thing, put up with the little brats when she had to, and have a great time on the slopes.

So the Skinny Rabbit Bride said yes to the ski trip. She didn't have a clue about what was in store for her. That Skinny Rabbit Bride was about to turn velveteen . . . and find another trail. The Great Stag was calling to her.

As Becky got in the bus for the ski trip, there was her sorority sister, Kay, who was so genuinely nice. There was the Young Life leader who didn't even know her but who really seemed to appreciate her coming on the trip at the last moment. And then there was Amy. Amy was one of the children Becky was stuck with to share a cabin.

Although Amy was young, she was not a child. She was sixteen and within a curled eyelash of being as drop-dead beautiful as Becky. In fact, anyone but Becky herself may have thought Amy beat her by an eyelash. That alone would have been enough to turn Becky off to this girl, but there was also something else. Something very different about this high-school kid. Amy was a Young Life campaigner, meaning she wasn't there just for the ski trips and clubs. Amy loved skiing and having fun, of course, and she jumped right into the middle of it all. But she also took her faith seriously. She went to Bible studies with the Young Life leader's wife, and she had made a serious commitment to Jesus. *She talked about Him so personally on the bus trip—like he was* real *or something,* thought Becky.

This combination of fun and energy and life and faith on the bus trip across country creeped Becky out a little bit. She'd never been around so many Christians who took their faith so seriously. But hey, she could shake it off. It was almost time to hit the slopes.

On the first night in their cabin, all the counselors were given a sheet with discussion questions centered around the talk that the Young Life leader had just given. (Becky was twenty minutes late to the man's talk. They hardly gave a girl time to do her makeup!)

As she sat in that rustic lodge with high wooden rafters, it rattled her to be around so many committed

Christians. Literally dozens of counselors her age were there, people who didn't worry about blow-drying their hair. People who laughed at the skits and sang from their hearts. And who had actually listened during the talk.

The next thing she knew, someone was calling her name. It was discussion time, and Becky was called on to lead the discussion. Surprised, she grabbed a Bible from the stack in the corner. Then she stopped, unsure of what to do next. Apparently they expected her to know where something called *Second Chronicles* was. What in the world was a *chronicle*, anyway? Her first thought was that her Dad might have driven one at one time.

Slowly it dawned on her: Chronicles must be a book somewhere in her oversized Bible. Becky had barely remembered at the very last minute even to grab her Bible. She'd never actually *read* the thing. How was she supposed to know where to find a chronicle? She thumbed the early pages, assuming she could find it alphabetically. But she quickly realized that whoever laid this book out didn't *bother* to alphabetize the books.

The tension mounted as she riffled through those incredibly thin pages, all sticking together because they'd never been opened. That's when Amy came to her rescue.

"Hey, Becky, I beat you there! Can I read the verse?" The look of relief on Becky's face met a warm smile on Amy's. And soon it was Amy who gently, patiently guided the discussion. It was Amy who even asked if Becky minded her closing their time in prayer at the end.

Mind? No, Becky didn't mind. Not at all.

If Amy suspected Becky had almost been exposed, she didn't act like it. Instead she acted as if she liked Becky. That made it tough for Becky to get to sleep that night.

On the first day on the slopes, Becky hit the first Black Diamond trail, and she was gone the rest of the day. The next day, however, Amy and Becky shared the same ski lift on their first run of the morning. It would be the first of many chair-lift seats they would share that day. Not only could Amy keep up with Becky on the slopes, she was light years ahead of the older girl when it came to being real. Becky was amazed that Amy was just a high-school girl. She was so deep. So . . . *real*.

In the next three days Becky got over her resentment of Amy's rival looks, and she got used to Amy's maturity and depth. She even came to appreciate it. The result: the two girls became the best of friends.

On the last night of a Young Life camp, there is often a "Say So." That's a time when the high-school kids have an opportunity to stand up and share what God has done in their lives in the past week or the past year. Some shared how they'd wandered away from their faith and how this trip or a friend or a Young Life Club back home had brought them back to Jesus. What brought the biggest cheers, however, were those who shared how this was the very first time they learned that Jesus was real. That He had been born and lived and died on the cross, all for them. And that by asking Jesus into their lives, they could become new and clean . . . and real.

Becky was one of the last to stand up—a counselor, of all things, standing up and sharing that a kid in her room had changed her life. Actually, they had all changed her life in the way they had loved and accepted her at a level she'd never known. But it was Amy, Becky told them, who had asked her a crucial question earlier that day on the slopes.

As the two girls sat together, swaying and kicking their skis on the long ride up the lift, Amy asked Becky if she had ever asked Jesus to come into her heart. In tears, Becky finally came clean—not just to Amy but to God. She admitted she didn't really know Jesus. But she wanted to know Him with all her heart. Amy prayed with Becky right there on the ski lift, and the two of them hugged, sixty feet above the slopes. They were so preoccupied that when the lift came to an end, they got their skis tangled and fell on top of each other. But instead of being embarrassed, Becky laughed. For the first time in a long, long time, it didn't matter how she looked. It didn't even matter that she fell in front of others.

Becky had held back until last to share that night

because she had no idea how people would take a counselor being led to Jesus by a kid. But those people didn't judge her; they mobbed her. The girls and the other kids and the counselors and the Young Life leader and his wife were suddenly hugging and crying with her. It was a real rush—light-years beyond any thrill of conquest Becky had known before.

Because of the love from all the Wise Hunters on that trip, Becky met the One who could really change her life. The One whose love could make her *real.*

That night a Skinny Rabbit Bride disappeared. And a Great Stag and a Velveteen Rabbit were in the room, full of people who cheered for a young woman who had finally become real.

NO MORE SKINNY RABBIT BRIDE

Yes, Becky's life was changed on that Young Life ski trip. So changed that all the way home, the engagement ring on her finger seemed to itch and burn. Carrying that ring on that fourteen-hour bus trip back to the college from camp was Becky's journey from the Shire to Mount Doom. She didn't have to face armies of Orcs or dark wizards or balrogs breathing fire to get there; like Frodo's One Ring, the ring she wore unleashed dark visions of doubt, telling her that what had happened on the ski lift and at the lodge last night wasn't *really* real. This was nothing more than a bunch of high-school kids on a ski trip. It was all manipulation of her emotions. It was all just talk meant to delude the weak or gullible. When school started again, her psychology professors would blow huge holes through what had happened at that camp.

But Becky knew in her heart that none of her doubts were true. After all, she was a master manipulator. She *knew* manipulation. This Jesus was real. And she knew that what He had done in coming into her life was real as well. So real, in fact, that after sleeping for fourteen hours after getting back home, she woke up and made the two-hour drive to her fiancé's home.

She arrived unannounced and unexpected. And at a fast-food restaurant near the young man's house, they sat and had a soda. She confessed to him what had happened. Not just at camp—the whole story. And finally, in one of the longest stretches of her life, she reached across the table and handed the ring to him.

In many ways it was like Frodo's struggle at the very end of his journey—wanting to keep the ring instead of throwing it into the fires. She wanted to keep it. She had *earned* it. It was her *precious*, her only reward for chasing down that long Skinny Rabbit Trail. But she also knew that she had obtained that ring by the foulest of means. And she was not going to marry this fine man or anyone else until she became real . . . as real as Jesus' love promised to make her.

So Becky and her fiancé broke up that day.

And here's where I get to say: "And now . . . the *rest* of the story."

Two years after Becky graduated, there was a wedding in her hometown. It was an extremely muggy, early July evening. And at this wedding . . . Becky was the bride, and Amy a bridesmaid. And the groom? None other than the boy to whom Becky had handed back the ring. Only now she wasn't a Skinny Rabbit Bride. She was now a Wise Hunter. After all, she had found her Great Stag, Jesus.

It wasn't all easy. Becky had spent the two years since they broke up working on herself. Asking the hard questions about her actions. Humbly learning from Wise Hunters the ways of Jesus and how to treat other people. She even became a Young Life Club leader her first year out of college.

It wasn't always easy, giving up that heady rush of the Skinny Rabbit Trail she'd followed for so long. But she'd learned that such power and ego trips led nowhere but to pits of emptiness and loneliness, not to mention the guilt of leading all those others into pits of crushed hopes and dreams.

God smiled on her and caused her path to cross once again with the man she would marry. A man she couldn't wait to marry. A man she would pledge to love for all her life—and *mean it.*

This was the happiest day of her life—the Skinny Rabbit Bride had seen the Wise Hunters . . . and followed them. Becky's story reminds us that there is a way back from the longest Skinny Rabbit Trail or the stickiest, deepest pit.

That's what we'll explore in depth in the next chapter.

8
WISE HUNTERS
TO THE RESCUE

Picture yourself on the trail of the Great Stag. You've trained for this moment long and hard, hunting lesser prey, spending many hours conditioning yourself for the long chase. And finally it is all paying off. You're not far behind the stag; you've pulled far ahead of the other hunters. Your steed is running steady, and your energy is high.

Your eyes wander over the landscape. Up ahead on the right, you catch a quick glimpse of a rabbit disappearing into the woods. You think, *Hmmmm. That rabbit is not more than twenty paces off the main road and down a little embankment—it's really not that far. And I'm so far ahead of the others; I can easily snag that rabbit and be back on the stag trail long before they catch up.*

You veer off to the right. You dismount and jog through a stretch of tall weeds to where the rabbit disappeared into the brush. You enter the brush and see the little critter disappear again into the trees ahead. You're close. You plunge headlong toward the rabbit, forgetting everything around you. You're about to close in. In moments you will have it hanging from your belt and be back on the road.

Suddenly you find yourself slipping down a steep embankment, and when you land, you are up to your hips in a thick, gooey slime.

You look around. You're in a pit of the black stuff, enclosed by steep dirt walls five feet high. No problem. You'll just wade to the nearest wall and crawl out. But the goo is so thick, you can't move your legs forward. You try to lift your foot, but it's a slow, arduous, almost impossible process.

Maybe I can pull myself along with my hands, you think. So you put your left hand into the stuff and try to paddle. But the hand sticks. You use your right hand to try to pull out your left, but it, too, becomes gunked up with the black stuff.

You hear a distant shout as the second hunter goes past. You pull with all your might, and your left hand comes free, but it trails long strings of the goo. You try to wipe it off on your shirt, sticking your hand to your shirt. You hear the shout of the third hunter as he goes by.

Now you're frantic. You're off the road, so no one sees you. And you're not sure you want to be seen. This is pure embarrassment. *I can handle this*, you tell yourself.

But the more you twist and turn to get out of this mess, the more stuck you get. You grit your teeth. *I know I'm strong enough to get out of this!* You try with all your might to move toward the bank, but it's useless. Hunters four, five, six, and seven rush by on the road above you. You soon realize you need help. This little side trip is not only going to cost *you*, but it's also going to cost someone else his precious time and energy to get you out of this mess.

Finally, in desperation you call out, "Help me!" From the roadway above, an agile, muscular hunter hears your cry and leaves his own quest to follow the sound. You look up and see him looking down at you in pity; he is a strong, wise-looking hunter with graying hair and a deep tan.

You tell him what happened, but he already seems to know. "I've been here before, my friend," he says. Without a word, he produces a vial from his pack. He lays a couple of logs on the surface of the black gunk, crawls on them to where you're stuck, and pours an oily substance over your hands, freeing them from the tar. Then he goes back to the bank, finds a strong limb, extends it for you to grasp, and with his great strength pulls you from the pit.

Then he pours the vial over your legs and cleans the tar from them. He gives it to you, and you clean the rest yourself. You look down at your legs and see fresh pink scars from where the tar was stuck to your skin. Your hands are scarred as well.

"Come on!" the hunter says. "We must get back in the hunt." He jogs back to the road and mounts his charger, and you also remount and follow close behind. As he crests a little rise just ahead, you see that his legs are lacerated with dark, permanent scars. Yet as you watch, he surges forward and is soon leading the way. You are no longer in the lead, but you are grateful to the hunter that you are at least back on the quest. In fact, you find it sort of comforting to know that you have someone strong and wise to follow, someone who knows the trail, the pitfalls, and the ways of the Great Stag.

And so you press on.

WE NEED WISE HUNTERS

Sin will entice you off the path and take you places you don't want to go, and often those places are sticky pits that are hard to get out of. If you do happen to fall into one of these pits, the temptation is to be prideful and think, *I can get out of this myself.*

In reality, you're not only stuck; you're embarrassed. You don't want to expose your failure to others, but you are lost unless you get over that terrible pride and simply call out for help. When you do, you'll almost always find help from someone who has already been through what you're going through—someone who can help you get back in the quest. James says, "Therefore confess your sins to each other and pray for each other so that you may be healed" (James 5:16).

Everyone needs a Wise Hunter to depend on and follow. A mentor, a strong Christian, a person who has been there and done that. These are the types of people you want to find and to follow. Not only because they can lead you off of Skinny Rabbit Trails and lift you out of pits, but also because once you're back in the race, they'll lead the way to the Great Stag, the real life you've been longing for.

THE WAY OF THE WISE HUNTER

If you were lost, would you rather have a confusing map or a personal guide? Duh! Maps can be as hard to read as they are to fold. A Wise Hunter is one who knows the way. He or she is someone who will come alongside you and is consistently committed to your finding your very best. A Wise Hunter is someone who walks with a kind of confidence that comes from having led others well. Wise Hunters have figured out that life works best when people stay on the track of their quest and don't get led astray. This track may be long, arduous, and sometimes tiring, but it leads to life and purpose and to waking up every morning without regret over the night before.

The best thing about a Wise Hunter—and the thing

that makes him or her a dependable help and guide—
is the fact that Wise Hunters do not depend on themselves for their knowledge and wisdom. They have
learned the trails and pits and bogs from someone far
above themselves, whose ways and wisdom are absolutely infallible.

When you choose a mentor for yourself, it's crucial to
be sure this person does not depend solely on his or her
own wisdom, experience, and ability, valuable as those
attributes may be. You want to be sure that your mentor-
helper is depending on nothing less than God Himself.

The psalmist David is a dependable guide and mentor for all of us. David was a Wise Hunter who defended
his sheep from lions and other predators. Yet he followed more than his share of Rabbit Trails and fell into
his share of pits. But every time he got into trouble, he
found God to be his dependable guide and mentor.

In one of David's most famous and helpful psalms,
he used the image of a shepherd to tell us what it's like
to follow God. In Psalm 23, he shows us the benefits,
provisions, and protections we receive when we submit
to God's guidance and leadership.

The LORD is my shepherd, I shall not be in want.

A good and valid mentor and guide will always point
you toward God, whom David calls his Shepherd. A good

mentor and guide serves God the Shepherd by helping keep His sheep on the path—a path of provision. If your mentor serves God, he or she will lead you toward more of what can really nourish your health, your home, your heart, and your faith.

A mentor and guide can be a friend, a spouse, or a coworker. What you must have is someone who helps keep you on track with God's purpose and moves you toward God's very best for your life.

He makes me lie down in green pastures,
he leads me beside quiet waters.

No matter how intense the pursuit of the goal, everyone needs peace, rest, and reflection. When was the last time you really felt rested? Be honest. Do you think rest is even an option in your life? One of the hallmarks of life today is *rush*. None of us is immune to the hassle of too much to do and not enough time to do it.

Two things are needed to get out of this trap. First, we need a time-out. We must take real time to step off the hamster wheel long enough to replenish our energy and recenter our lives. Second, when the press of the hectic rush is unavoidable, we need to learn to experience peace even when we can't avoid being in the middle of chaos.

Impossible, you think. Not at all. You can reach the

point where you stand in the pushing, aggravated crowds during the Christmas rush and actually feel as though you're standing in David's green pastures and beside quiet waters. It's not a trick. When you rest in all that God has given you to enable you to grow (green pastures), beside the life-giving water that quiets your heart, you can have peace, even in the longest of checkout lines.

He restores my soul.
He guides me in paths of righteousness
for his name's sake.

Good mentors are those who take you to this good Shepherd of whom David speaks. We know Him, of course, as Jesus. He is the One who can restore your soul and help you keep your life on the path of righteousness. In the Bible the word *righteousness* literally means *to stay between the lines.* The promise of the psalm is that God will keep you *between the lines.* What does this mean?

Think about driving home from work. What keeps us safe and gets us where we want to go? Staying between the lines painted on the road keeps us safe. Good mentors will follow Jesus, who guides all in paths of righteousness, keeping us between the lines as we move toward our best . . . which is His best for us.

Even though I walk
through the valley of the shadow of death,
I will fear no evil,
for you are with me;
your rod and your staff,
they comfort me.

God is there for you even as you face death itself. Those words are easy to read sitting in the comfort of your den. But what if you're in Iraq, riding into Tikrit or Fallujah with the Third Marines or First Infantry Division? On every patrol there's a chance you'll be hit with IEDs or snipers with armor-piercing rounds. There is always the chance of a mortar round being lobbed at random into your camp. Is it realistic to think that God is there for you when facing such terrors as these? How about the very real terror of cancer or some other life-threatening disease?

He is. And a good mentor can lead you to know it. He or she can lead you to the arms of God, a place where you will find true comfort, for Jesus knows firsthand what you're going through. He has been there . . . faced the worst. He died and rose again to open for us a pathway out of fear and to fill us with peace in our deepest hearts and souls, even in the very face of death.

Recently I had the great honor of speaking at a conference for faculty and staff couples at West Point. Most of these warriors had already been deployed at least once. Yet their faith, courage, and commitment were incredible. Fourteen months in a war zone has a way of exposing all the Skinny Rabbit Trails that look so tempting here at home. They had learned it's the Shepherd's path that offers real help and hope in the dark and threatening times.

> *You prepare a table before me*
> *in the presence of my enemies.*
> *You anoint my head with oil;*
> *my cup overflows.*

Right in the midst of conflict, God provides for you. Often He uses His servants to supply the help you need. And when this happens, you'll discover there really is Someone who loves you for yourself. Talk about an overflowing feeling of finally being "home." Being whole. Being really valued. It happens when you know that you are deeply loved just as you are.

> *Surely goodness and love will follow me*
> *all the days of my life,*
> *and I will dwell in the house of the LORD forever.*

God uses mentors as His tools, His messengers, and His servants to help keep you on a path of goodness, love, and blessing for the rest of your days. As we saw in Becky's story, all those conditional, short-term, guilt- and shame-producing Skinny Rabbit relationships we experience in life have a way of erasing any sense of permanence.

Sadly, Becky's story is not all that unusual. And unfortunately, stories like hers rarely have a happy ending. We've all seen marriages fail after thirty-five years. Seen huge companies fold and colossal towers crumble. Some have seen death snatch away a loved one far too soon. All this makes it hard to believe anything in our world is permanent.

But good mentors who follow God lead you to the one thing that *is* secure in a world filled with danger and loss: a real path to green pastures and life-giving water. These mentors lead you to Someone who will stand by your side and fight for you, to Someone who has said, "Never will I leave you; never will I forsake you" (Heb. 13:5).

Never. Not at all. *Nunca*. It's a picture of help and companionship on the path toward your real reward. It's genuine security in an insecure world.

HOW TO BE A WISE HUNTER

When we're trapped in a pit, all our focus is on our plight and how to get out of it. But after Wise Hunters have rescued us and set us back on the right path, most of us want to become Wise Hunters ourselves.

So how do you do that? How do you find out what is real and begin following after things that really count and lead to real life?

One way you can learn to be a Wise Hunter yourself is to look at the lives of those who have followed the paths of Great Stags. One such person is Albert Lexie. You may not have heard of Albert (relatively few have), but he's way ahead of most of us when it comes to spotting and following what's real. As you read about his story, think about the paths God puts in front of you that can lead to your being real as well.

Albert Lexie isn't a doctor or nurse or specialist. But Albert gets on a bus very early three days a week, every week, during the dead of winter or the heat of summer, and takes a ride of almost two hours (counting transfers) to Children's Hospital of Pittsburgh. Albert doesn't use state-of-the-art machines to heal or help, but he does a ton of healing while he's there.

It started one night more than two decades ago when Albert was watching television. Children's Hospital was conducting its annual telethon. Sick kids needed help, and Albert's heart was touched. The next day he took the bus to the hospital for the first time. He handed a surprised receptionist an envelope containing his entire life's savings: almost seven-hundred and fifty dollars. But Albert couldn't shake the feeling that there was more he could do for these kids. So he got on the bus, went back another day, and convinced administrators at the hospital to let him help by doing what he knew he did well—set up a shoe-shine stand and shine shoes. Only this time, his hands and strength would benefit the kids: *Albert's kids.*

Each day Albert is at the hospital, he makes people's shoes look brighter and better, and then he walks down the halls and talks or sings with the sick kids to make them feel better and to brighten their lives. The ones he chooses to visit most often are the sickest of the sick with the very least hope of ever going home. He uses his songs and words and prayers to do the best he can to help them out of pits of despair and bogs of hopelessness. Shining one shoe at a time, Albert Lexie has donated more than $110,000 to the hospital.

One day U.S. Congressman John Kasich interviewed Albert, who had won the 1997 Jefferson Medal for Outstanding Citizens and later won the prestigious 2006 National Caring Award. When asked by Kasich what it was that motivated him on those cold, cold winter mornings to show up and shine shoes, Lexie replied that he could sing the reason better then he could explain it.

"Go ahead," the congressman urged Albert.

So right there, surrounded by television cameras, doctors, administrators, sick kids, assorted government

officials, and other city leaders, Albert sang about the
Greatest Hunter of all, who came to pull us out of any
bog or pit and to put our feet on high places. He sang the
old, old, song . . .[1]

On a hill far away stood an old, rugged cross,
The emblem of suffering and shame . . .[2]

Wise Hunters like Albert Lexie know how to be
there for others because they're following a man named
Jesus who gave His all to be there for lost and hurting
people.

Wise Hunters are like that. A Wise Hunter can be
your aunt, who always loved you and always will. He's
that youth leader who didn't give up on you. He's the
corpsman who kept shaking you and telling you to keep
your eyes open, that you were going to make it home.
She's the teacher who saw something in you when all
the others were telling you that you had marginal talent.
He's that friend who was always so steady and real.
Often they're people you might have missed or walked
right past because they're the ones shining your shoes,
making you look and feel better—not promising you
they can triple your money overnight.

Wise Hunters are servants of others. Plain and
simple. They get their eyes off of themselves (and off
Skinny Rabbit Trails) and see the needs of others. For

the path of service and sacrifice leads toward that old rugged cross—and toward a life of clarity and purpose. So wherever you are today, emotionally or geographically, know two things.

First, you are not alone—even if you think you are. God has placed Wise Hunters near you. People who may have achieved great fame or be as unknown as a shoe-shine man in a children's hospital, sharing in common a servant's heart. Find them. Enlist their help. Depend on them. Follow their ways, and they can lead you on a path to your goal and help you stay on it.

And second, always make it your aim to become a Wise Hunter yourself. One way to do that is to seek a path that actively involves you in helping others look better, feel better, and move toward health and life. You may get your hands stained in the process, but nail-scarred hands have done it all for us—they point toward the way, the truth, and the life that can give us and others wisdom, guidance, and strength.

9
LEARNING TO BE STILL: THE KEY TO FOLLOWING THE PATH OF PEACE

The young hunter hurried along the trail, weary and swaying in the saddle but doggedly determined. It was his first hunt for the Great Stag. He was not yet as skilled or as strong and conditioned as other hunters, and thus many were far ahead of him. But what he lacked in skill and experience he made up for in hard work. He forced himself to ride harder and longer than the others. He kept going well into the night, when other hunters had stopped to enjoy a little rest by their warm campfires.

One day as he rounded a bend, he saw an older hunter standing perfectly still beside the trail as his horse grazed nearby. The young hunter could not understand this. As he approached, he asked, "Why have you stopped? Don't you know there's a long trail ahead, and the Great Stag is always running?"

"Be still," replied the Wise Hunter. "I'm listening."

"Listening for what?" asked the young hunter.

"For the sound of the Great Stag's hooves. For the screech of birds fleeing from its path. For the cries of animals getting out of its way. You can often know where the Great Stag is if you stop and listen for the signs. But to do that, you must learn to be still."

From that Wise Hunter, the young hunter learned that the best way to pursue your goal is not always to run long hours at full pace. Sometimes we need to stop, be still, and get our bearings. Running long and hard does a hunter no good if he has veered off onto a Rabbit Trail.

For an example of someone who has not yet learned this vital lesson, let's visit our friends Elmer and Eloise again. The Smudleys are still frazzled, chasing Skinny Rabbits down random trails. Let's look in to see where the chase leads them.

Elmer rushed home—picking up a bake-it-yourself pepperoni pizza on the way. This was the beginning of Thursday Night Ballet, a well-choreographed, well-rehearsed blending of four schedules into a multilayered dance of precision timing. Art in motion, it was.

Elmer, the choreographer, opened the performance with a ring of the doorbell at 6:34 p.m. The melodic *ding dong* was the signal for Eloise, who stood ready to pirouette into the kitchen and open the door to the oven (which had been preheated to 450 degrees for ten minutes).

Elmer promenaded into the kitchen at 6:35 p.m. With a quick yet heartfelt kiss to Eloise at 6:36, and hellos and hugs to Bobby and Betsy at 6:37, he slid the pizza onto the middle rack of the oven and set the timer for twenty-three minutes.

Elmer checked his atomic-precision watch. He had committed this routine to memory after mapping it out meticulously on a spreadsheet in his computer. So exact was the timing that one little misstep would collide the four schedules, which would trip over each other and collapse in an exploding fireball of chaos.

However, from the very start, Elmer's schedule had run like clockwork.

Until this fateful night.

At 6:42, Betsy (dressed in her pink leotard for dance class at 7:15) and Bobby (dressed for his soccer game at 7:20) both helped set the dinner table for Dad, who was dressed in business casual for a debt-free seminar at the Marriott at 7:30.

At 6:45, Bobby went to his room to feed his gerbil some sunflower seeds. That's when something went horribly, awfully, terribly wrong.

The first inkling came at 6:46, when Eloise announced that she couldn't find her music for choir practice. As she searched the house, Elmer was put in charge of the pizza. No problem. He was flexible.

At 6:52, Elmer looked out the window and noticed the minivan's tire was flat. This mishap could throw off the schedule by as much as seven minutes! If he pumped up the tire right now, he would still have one minute to spare before the pizza was ready.

Elmer headed out to the garage for the tire pump, but on the way he noticed Bobby turning green. "What's wrong?" Elmer asked his son. Bobby admitted he had ingested a funny-looking pepperoni he plucked from the pizza. He was turning greener by the second. Elmer told Bobby to lie down, then rushed on out to the garage.

But in his sickly state, Bobby had forgotten to close the gerbil cage.

Tension built in the garage. Elmer couldn't find the tire pump. He lost ten precious minutes throwing aside tools and upending boxes. "Ah! There it is!" The pump had been dropped behind Grandpa's moose head. It was 7:03, three minutes *past* the scheduled eating time.

The world was starting to tilt.

Elmer frantically disentangled the tire pump from the moose antlers and sprinted out to the van like a pit-crew member at the Indy 500. He pumped up the tire as fast and as furiously as he could.

7:07. The gerbil escaped its cage.

7:10. First gerbil sighting. Toodles the Poodle chased the runaway rodent through the rec room. Betsy tried to grab the little critter but tripped over a cord and broke a lamp, which cut her arm.

7:11. Elmer came back in the house to see Betsy crying, her arm bleeding. Elmer always wanted to be the hero of the family—but he got dizzy at the sight of blood. He rushed to the bathroom medicine cabinet to grab some smelling salts for himself and bandages for Betsy, who was now late for her dance class.

7:13. Eloise—who had just found her music under a stack of mail in the office—entered the living room, where she found bleeding Betsy, barfing Bobby, and . . .

7:14. Second gerbil sighting. On Eloise's foot. She screamed.

7:15. Elmer, still a bit shaky, returned to the living room to check on Eloise and pass out bandages. The smoke alarm went off. Loudly. It was hard to hear anything over the piercing blast. Elmer ran to the kitchen and opened the oven. Smoke billowed out.

7:17. Elmer bravely extinguished the pepperoni fire with a bag of flour, which settled like a soft, light snow all over the kitchen.

7:18. Everybody coughed—including the gerbil that ran over Eloise's ankle. Eloise screamed again. Betsy cried. Bobby threw up. Elmer fainted. And somewhere behind this scene hopped a Skinny Rabbit, innocently unaware of the chaos it was leaving in its path.

FINDING THE PATH OF PEACE

If ever a family needed to find a path to peace, it's the Smudleys. Or maybe it's your family. Instead of the continual crisis and confusion of following Rabbit Trails, families caught up in the frenzy of overloaded schedules desperately need a path to peace to center their lives and stabilize their worlds. That path is increasingly harder to find in a world in which nanoseconds count and life is continually so loud that we have trouble coping with real quiet. We even need *white noise* just to go to sleep.

Maybe this is why God told David, "Be still, and know that I am God" (Ps. 46:10). It's hard for us to be still. Frankly, it's hard even to see the point of it. In our lives today it doesn't make sense because it's just the opposite of what we need to keep pace with the scramble of schedules. But sooner or later our ballet, like the Smudleys', will end in disaster. The dancers will entangle themselves and crash to the stage. Then the need to be still will become apparent. Then we will see the need for a mentor, a guide, a Wise Hunter who can lead us to the path of peace. We will need someone who has discovered what it means to *be still*.

QUIET MERCIES

Mary Ann's story demonstrates what can happen when a guide or mentor helps you learn to be still.

I grew up knowing that I was different, and I hated it. I was born with a cleft palate, and when I started school, my classmates made it clear to me how I must look to others; I was a little girl with a misshapen lip, crooked nose, lopsided teeth, and garbled speech.

When schoolmates asked, "What happened to your lip?" I'd tell them I'd fallen and cut it on a piece of glass. Somehow it seemed more acceptable to have suffered an accident than to have been born different. I was convinced that no one outside my family could ever love me. Or even like me. Then I entered Mrs. Leonard's second-grade class.

Mrs. Leonard was round and pretty and fragrant, with shining brown hair and warm, dark, smiling eyes. Everyone adored her. But no one came to love her more than I did. And for a special reason.

The time came for the annual hearing tests given at our school. I could barely hear out of one ear and was not about to reveal something else that would single me out as different. So I cheated.

The "whisper test" required each child to go to the classroom door, turn sideways, and close one ear with a finger while the teacher whispered something from her desk, which the child repeated. Then the same for the other ear. Nobody checked how tightly the untested ear was covered, so I merely pretended to block mine.

As usual, I was last. But all through the testing I wondered what Mrs. Leonard might say to me. I knew from previous years that the teacher whispered things like "The sky is blue" or "Do you have new shoes?"

My time came. I turned my bad ear toward her, plugging up the other just enough to be able to hear. I waited, and then came the words that God had surely put into her mouth, seven words that changed my life forever.

Mrs. Leonard, the teacher I adored, said softly, "I wish you were my little girl."[1]

You can see how these few words calmed the inner turmoil in this troubled girl's heart and allowed her to be still. This wise woman who was her teacher changed her life. Her wisdom and care put Mary Ann on the path to peace.

Being still is a state of peace in God—a peace that gives you supernatural calm in the middle of burning pizzas, fainting dads, and coughing gerbils, even in the turmoil of uncertainty about your own value. It's as much a mind-set as an actual action. It's what the Bible calls the peace that passes all understanding, a peace that guards your heart and your mind.

Are you ready to sign up for that kind of peace?

Many Wise Hunters will tell you that one way it comes is by having a regular *be still* appointment with the God who created you—a short, specific time when you take the world off the hook and take a respite with the One who knit your heart and soul together while you were yet in your mother's womb. It is a time to read His book (it's a bestseller). It's a time to talk with Him like you would a friend (He is that!), sing a song to Him (yes, even with your voice), and worship Him (He's worthy of it). And maybe most importantly, it's a time to listen to Him.

But who has that kind of time? You have deadlines, commitments, and responsibilities. Contemplate the irony of saying that: you're too busy for God, who can give you what you need to deal with the busyness in your life. But irony or not, I understand the question. So I want to give you a few practical ways to put some *be still* into every day.

First let's take a closer look at Psalm 46:10: "Be still, and know that I am God."

Be still . . . Find a place of retreat and get quiet. I'm not talking forever. Maybe four minutes as you have your Wheat Chex and blueberries, or five minutes on the subway train, or seven minutes after the last kid is finally down and you've brushed your teeth and fallen into a chair in the bedroom, exhausted.

. . . *and know* . . . You're about to learn something. Listen!

. . . *that I* . . . The focus for these few minutes is God, not you, not your troubles.

. . . *am God* . . . This is the ultimate goal—a divine

connection with the Creator who made you and cares for you. The One who does know all about your troubles and has wisdom and counsel and life to give you.

Note also that *He* is God, not you. You don't have to do God's job for Him. Your job is to "trust and obey" as the old song tells us. He takes care of the rest. Not to hurt your feelings, but God doesn't *need* you to do anything for Him. Amazingly, He can actually accomplish things without you. We get in this mode of saying, "I'm doing this for God!" which is great unless you're trying to perform to get God's attention.

You know what God really wants? He wants *you*. Not your performance. He wants to spend time with you. And He wants you to say yes to the good things for you and others. He wants to keep your life between the lines. Not because He's a controlling dictator but because He's a loving Lord, and obedience to God is following His path . . . which just happens to run through peace, hope, health, rest, and real life (see Deuteronomy 30). We fight so hard to get off course and go chasing after Skinny Rabbits. He patiently waits for us to finally stop running or until we're finally forced to be still in a bog or a pit.

Picture yourself running around from work to home to school to the store to softball practice to dance class to piano lessons to home to work to school to . . . oblivion. You're worn-out. Frazzled.

Now picture yourself getting on a plane and taking

off. Soon you're flying high over your city. Very quickly the *big* world, the *big* problems, the *big* busyness you left on the ground below all look very *small*. From your higher perspective you begin to see a truly bigger world.

That's exactly what happens when you spend *be still* time with God. When you're on God's lap as He sits on His throne, your problems down here look pretty puny. When you get in His presence, your perspective changes. Your vision changes. And that's where your future changes because now you see what's truly important—Him. Him above all. And as He whispers in your ear, you hear words of comfort, love, life, and belonging; when your feet are back on the ground, you remember the words of His dream for you, His child. And suddenly, nothing else seems as important—or as impossible—as it once did.

Here's another picture. While walking though the woods, you discover a beautiful little pond nestled in the trees. You pick up a rock that fits snugly in your hand and pitch it into the water. The rock makes a deeply satisfying *ka-lunk* and spreads ripples across the surface. When the water is churned up, your focus is on the rippling waves—on the movement. But when the water calms down, when the water is quiet, it reflects. And things become clearer. You can see *into* the water.

When your life is churned up with busyness and worry, it's easy to focus on the frantic movements of problem solving and keeping things going. These are the things that grab your attention. But when you can be still before God, you can see your own reflection better—a reflection of who you are in Him. And you can see more clearly and deeply into your situation as well.

Instead of water all churned up with worry and constant activity, you stand beside still water (see Ps. 23:2), which enables you to see clearly enough to be still and know your God. Even a short time of stillness with Him can calm your life, making direction and decisions so much clearer.

"Be still and know that I am God." When you're still, you can see God Himself. You can hear His whisper. You begin to sense the difference between what's urgent and what's important. That's a lot of benefit for just slowing down your life for a short time to be still.

While you're in God's presence, if you think through difficult choices ahead of you, you'll be better prepared for whatever challenges you have to face. Choices become clearer when you think things through with God.

For instance, you may decide one morning, "I am no longer going to gossip," or "I'm not going to do any more impulse buying." You've been down those Skinny Rabbit Trails and gotten stuck in bogs before. Then afternoon comes, and you're suddenly face-to-face with the temptation. Only this time you have a Wise Hunter standing with you and God's Spirit inside of you, reminding you,

"Didn't we just talk about this? Remember your decision this morning? Didn't you ask Me for the strength to walk the other way when the gossip starts flying at work?"

You've already thought it through. Already prayed it through. Already been still for a few minutes to let life settle down and let God's Word reflect on your life situation. Now, when faced with temptation, that stillness revisits you, reminding you of the path of peace you saw from high up in God's perspective. And suddenly you see the temptation for what it is: a Rabbit Trail leading to nothing that can nourish you and the danger of a bog at the end.

There are several other wonderful benefits to being still before God. Be still for just a few more pages and discover them!

FINDING TIME TO BE STILL

Let's say you actually do set four or even seven minutes aside to be still, right in the middle of deadlines and pressures and stresses. That's not a very long time to step off the hamster wheel—just one-tenth of a TV show. You can do it. Just stop. Shut the door. Take in those minutes of heaven. Seven minutes to be still. Seven minutes of just you and God.

Why does the time need to be scheduled? Simple. If you don't set your schedule in today's world, someone else will set it for you. So schedule a Take Seven every day—just like any other important appointment. If you're at work and fortunate enough to have an assistant, you can ask him or her to hold your calls during that time. You can even practice being still right in the midst of things blowing up or falling apart or in the middle of your normal busyness. You don't even have to shut your door once you learn how to do it.

When you need a burst of wisdom, when someone is counting on you for an answer right now, or when things are generally going nuts, *think a prayer to God.* There's a great little book on this subject—almost four hundred years old—called *The Practice of the Presence of God* by Brother Lawrence. This humble monk made a big discovery: he could be in God's presence anywhere! He learned how to find time with God as he mopped the floor or washed the dishes or took out the garbage.

In the book, Brother Lawrence writes that "there is not in the world a kind of life more sweet and delightful, than that of a continual conversation with God. Those only can comprehend it who practice and experience it."

Maybe you can't stop your busyness at just any time. But you can learn to be still, right in the middle of your busyness. Start by thinking a prayer to God. Actually look at the person in line ahead of you and say a quick prayer for him, stranger though he is. Thank the Lord for the traffic light you made it through . . . and for the four minutes you have to pray when you're stuck at the next one. When everything is chaos around you, even minutes with God or fleeting thoughts of Him can help you find rest.

Shutting the door for seven minutes and just thinking a prayer are only two ways for you to develop the habit of finding time with God in an out-of-time world. But really, you can find time to be still almost anytime, anywhere. You can start off your day with God. Ask for His advice on your commute to work. In the middle of your morning or your afternoon, take a refreshing walk with Him. (It worked for Adam!) On your way home, talk with Him about your day. Ask Him to help you avoid Skinny Rabbit Trails. Share your hopes and dreams with Him. And then *listen*. You just may hear Him share His hopes and dreams with you.

In addition to cultivating daily *be still* time by Taking Seven and Thinking Prayers, do one more thing: once every season, take a Be Still Day. It would be great if we all lived in the Little House on the Prairie and could take off every Sunday, all day. But the reality is, like my friend Tim Kimmel says, "Today we live in Little House on the Freeway!"

We live in a society today that has no edges or boundaries around work or shopping. But we can build the needed boundaries into our lives. When God designed you and me, He intended that we take off a day and rest. The original owner's manual actually said one day every *week*.

Now, don't shut this book!

God even showed us how to do it. After He created light and earth and heaven and stars and planets and galaxies and plants and animals and man, He took a day off: the Sabbath. God took a break. He didn't need it—but He knew we desperately would, so He modeled it for us.

Now, it's not impossible to move toward that goal of one day off per week. But don't set yourself up for failure by trying to make an abrupt, once-for-all decision to do it: "OK, I'm setting aside every Sunday as a sabbath day of rest for the rest of my life, starting right now!" Three weeks later, after messing up two Sundays in a row, you'll feel so guilty that you'll just conveniently forget the whole idea.

For many people, I suggest starting with a day each season on which they shut down the engines. *OK, it's winter. I'll find one slush day when I can get away with my God.* (It's OK for that day to be the span of time between when the kids go to school and when they come home). *At last, spring has sprung. I'm doing this Be Still Day outside! . . . Well, whaddaya know? It's summer already, and I'm gonna hide in that huge air-conditioned bookstore for the day, way in the back near the Raising Llamas section where (amazingly) few people go . . . Would you believe it's already fall? I'm going to ask my wife if she'll join me on this Be Still Day.*

It may be helpful for you to plan out and actually schedule your time to be still. I know, I know: life is full of lists and schedules and deadlines and calendars and meetings and appointments and pie charts and bar graphs and reports and timetables for the kids' sports and for relatives from out of state. The last thing you need is another list. I'm not talking about another list; I'm talking about making it a priority before the list fills up to put down a definite commitment for a time to be still.

One more thing: if you're looking for a great time and place to be still, no solution is better than to get in the habit of visiting your Father God's house at regular meeting times. Greet your brothers and sisters, share God stories, brag on your heavenly Father. Let the music and the focus on Jesus bring you far more than anything you bring Him, no matter how much you drop into the offering plate.

Once you've gotten started on a few minutes a day of be still time, and perhaps a day each season, maybe even a morning each week at an outstanding church, you're going to be hooked because of how much God brings to your life. And how much connecting to Him keeps you on the path of peace and off Rabbit Trails.

On at least one of those be still times, I suggest that you include your spouse, if you're married, or a best friend who really knows your heart. Spend some be still time together with that loved one or best friend. If your daily time with God is like gas in your car, be still time with your spouse is like putting racing fuel in your four-cylinder engine. It's amazing the wheelies you'll do with the extra energy and life you'll get as a couple!

All be still times give you great opportunities to evaluate your life, your schedule, and your future—to ask the deeper questions that usually get crowded out by a busy schedule. For example, you might ask God:

Who am I—how do You see me?
Where am I now in life?
Where do You want me to go?

Then ask the same questions as a couple:

Who are we—how do You see us?
Where are we now?
Where do You want us to go?

For your first be still time, why not start meditating on one of the best be still passages of the Bible, Psalm 46:1–11 (note how David's be still time occurs right in the middle of utter chaos):

God is our refuge and strength,
  an ever present help in trouble.
Therefore we will not fear, though the earth give way
  and the mountains fall into the heart of the sea,
though its waters roar and foam

and the mountains quake with their surging.
There is a river whose streams make glad the city
    of God,
    the holy place where the Most High dwells.
God is within her, she will not fall;
    God will help her at break of day.
Nations are in uproar, kingdoms fall;
    he lifts his voice, the earth melts.
The LORD Almighty is with us;
    the God of Jacob is our fortress.
Come and see the works of the LORD,
    the desolations he has brought on the earth.
He makes wars cease to the ends of the earth;
    he breaks the bow and shatters the spear,
    he burns the shields with fire.
"Be still, and know that I am God;
    I will be exalted among the nations,
    I will be exalted in the earth."
The LORD Almighty is with us;
    the God of Jacob is our fortress.

"Be still, and know that I am God." When you take time to be still, you're telling God that He's more important than the stuff swirling around you. Learn to be still, and the same Jesus who calmed the storm with just His voice can bring that peace that passes understanding into your heart.

10
HOW TO IDENTIFY
YOUR SKINNY RABBIT

When you're deep in the woods, thick with towering trees and deep underbrush, it's easy to become confused and lose track of your goal in the maze of other trails crisscrossing the forest. Some trails are well-worn, others barely discernible. Some are straight and easy to follow, while others twist and turn like pretzels. Some are wide through frequent usage, while others are narrow and seem seldom used.

Your goal, of course, is finding the Great Stag—the life, peace, and calm confidence I've called *rest*. It's the escape from the frenzy of wheel-spinning busyness. It's finding your passion and completion. It's finding your *home*, the place in which you were designed to fit into God's great scheme. In fact, it's finding God.

In that sense, the goal of the quest is common to all of us. We're all hunting the Great Stag. But that doesn't mean the Great Stag will lead us all to the same place.

One place to find life, peace, and rest is in a godly mate. Another is in service to others. Another is in meaningful work that contributes to the welfare of society and makes the world a better place. You can name hundreds of other places where people find life, peace, and rest. Where they find their passion—the thing God created them to do.

The variety of places we find God is one reason the quest can get so confusing. It's why we so easily get off on Rabbit Trails. We don't intentionally wander from our quest for the Great Stag, but we become uncertain about which trail leads to him. In other words, sometimes we don't follow the rabbit deliberately or because we're tempted by lesser, quicker, easier quarry than the Great Stag. Sometimes we chase Skinny Rabbits, thinking we're actually following the Great Stag. But we inadvertently got on the wrong trail.

How can we tell one trail from another? When trails fork and cross one another, how can we know we're staying on the right track and not following some Skinny Rabbit? How can we know up front that a goal we've chosen to pursue will be worthwhile? That it will work out? That when we finally reach the end of the trail, it won't lead us into a pit or bog?

How can you tell if this person you just started dating . . . this job you're in . . . this new ministry opportunity . . . or this career choice is a Skinny Rabbit? In

Matthew 7:16, Jesus gave us a way to tell: "By their fruit you will recognize them."

Here He was speaking specifically of false prophets, deceptive people who were not what they seemed to be. The principle is solid enough that it can apply to people, situations, or goals. You can judge any of these not by how they appear but by what they produce. A Skinny Rabbit produces nothing good for you. It's all bone and no meat. It has nothing nourishing, nothing worth the effort of the chase.

But if that wascally wabbit is out there in the brush, and all you see of him is a fleeting, blurry glimpse, and all you hear is an occasional rustle in the weeds, how

can you know he's a Skinny Rabbit before you put all your time and effort into the pursuit?

To help you, we have devised a Skinny Rabbit Detector. It's a device that helps you to determine whether what you're following is a Skinny Rabbit or a Great Stag. Take a person, possession, position, promotion, or place, and run it through this Skinny Rabbit Detector. Using this test, you can determine the truth up front so you won't be tempted to chase down the wrong trail.

If you're married, you may want to go through this detector with your spouse. It's an eye-opening way to open up dialog about your life and your days ahead.

Think of this little test as a chance for you to slow down. To step back. To be still for a moment. To take the time to look down the road a bit. Where is this road (or person, or job) leading you?

In some cases you may find the answers to these questions quite painful. You may be examining a trail that looks really good, and you really want to follow it. But grit your teeth and put that trail to the test before you take another step. What you learn could very well change your life. It might even save your life!

RABBIT DETECTOR INSTRUCTIONS

In the pages that follow are several sets of side-by-side questions that will help you to determine whether something (or someone) is worthy of pursuit. The questions to the left are labeled SR (Skinny Rabbit), and those on the right are labeled GS (Great Stag). Each question contains a blank space where you can insert the name of the person or item you are evaluating. Read the question, write in the blank the name of the person, place, or situation you're evaluating, and then think through, talk through, and pray through what you know about this person or goal. Then check whichever box describes the name in the blank. If your evaluation indicates that the check should go in the Great Stag box, check GS joyfully. If, on the other hand, your evaluation points toward the Skinny Rabbit box, don't cheat—check SR boldly and honestly. You do want the truth, don't you? Painful though the truth may be, it's better to find it now than at the sad end of a Skinny Rabbit Trail.

For example, let's say you're evaluating a person. Perhaps it's a certain friendship. Only, if you're honest, it may already be more than just a friendship. In your mind this person might, possibly, maybe could be *the one*. OK, put the one's name in the blanks of the questions in the side-by-side checklist. Evaluate each of the questions and place check marks in the boxes that best describe your friendship (OK, OK, so it's a *relationship*!). If you find in all honesty that the Skinny Rabbit statements best describe this person, then force yourself to check the SR boxes. If the Great Stag statements best describe this person, then check those boxes. If neither statement applies, leave both boxes blank. At the end, add up all the Skinny Rabbit boxes and all the Great Stag boxes.

What does this score tell you about this person? Does he or she lean toward being a Skinny Rabbit or a Great Stag? Pray and ask God what to do with your answers. If it's a job, decision, or situation that you need to evaluate, use the same questions and follow the same procedure.

What you write in the blanks should be those choices, decisions, or goals that have become really important to your life—the people or things that could lead you toward God or away from Him. To help you get started, here are some examples of the types of entries you could write in these blanks:

People
—your spouse (or boyfriend/girlfriend)
—your friends
—your associates
—your extended family

Possessions
—the things you surround yourself with
—the major purchase you just made
—the donation request you're considering

Positions

—your mind-set

—your place in your company or volunteer
organization

—how much time you spend at work

—whether to stay put or look for another job

Promotions

—the dreams you're pursuing

—that award you're after

Places

—the environment where you hang out

—your city, your home, your vacation spots

—that one *place* that defines success to you

—where you spend your holidays

While you're at it, why not work up the nerve to put yourself through the Skinny Rabbit Detector? Could you be someone else's Skinny Rabbit? As you read the questions, ask "How would my husband/wife answer this?" and "What would my enemies say?" Your goal is to find the truth.

SKINNY RABBIT DETECTOR

SR = Skinny Rabbit   **GS = Great Stag**

1. SR: ❑ Does _____ pull you away from your path of purpose, the progressive pursuit of a positive goal or dream? Is this person moving your life in a positive direction toward your goal? (Let's say you've wanted to be a veterinarian since you were six years old. Your parents were patient with you, even when they thought you were filling an ark with your animals. You are only ten college credits away from applying to vet school, and you're working hard to get there. Now you're in a relationship with someone who is allergic to cats, was bitten by a dog as a child, and is convinced all birds carry incurable diseases. He puts up with your "animal thing," but he's not in any way behind it.)

1. GS: ❑ Does _____ keep you on track with what you think is God's purpose for your life? Is this person moving you toward your goal or away from it? (Your friend isn't as animal happy as you are, but he's happy that you're so close to reaching your goal. He sets up study dates to help you when you have midterms. And he bought you that *America's Funniest Animals* video.)

2. SR: ❑ Does _____ emphasize the now, as in *right now*? (Does this person's actions shout, "Short-term! Eat, drink, and be merry, for tomorrow I'm moving on!"? Or if it's a decision or position you're fitting into this slot, does it hold short-term

2. GS: ❑ Is _____ able to delay gratification in order to achieve long-term goals? Does this person have patience and consider the long-term effects of his or her actions? What are the long-term rewards of following _____?

164

HOW TO IDENTIFY YOUR SKINNY RABBIT

SR = Skinny Rabbit

GS = Great Stag

(2. SR continued)
or long-term promise? What
are the long-term implications
of following _____?)

3. SR: ❑ Does _____ lead
you away from God? Does he
or she encourage you to act in
ways you know are contrary
to God's law?

3. GS: ❑ Does _____ lead
you into a deeper relationship
with God? Does he or she
behave in ways that make it
easier to do the right thing?

4. SR: ❑ Do you idolize
_____? Do you put _____
before God, God's people,
your family, or your *be still*
time?

4. GS: ❑ Does God come
before _____? Do you put
God's will before _____?

5. SR: ❑ Does _____ cause
you to defame, misuse, or
dishonor God's name?

5. GS: ❑ Does _____ lead
you to glorify and honor God
and His name in the way con-
versations are conducted?

6. SR: ❑ Does being with (or
being at, or doing) _____
exhaust you? (Do you often
leave this situation or person
with feelings of anxiety and
worry?)

6. GS: ❑ Does being with (or
being at, or doing) _____
energize you or make you feel
as though you're doing great
even if you're tired?

7. SR: ❑ Does _____ dis-
honor your parents or drive a
wedge between you and them?
*(WARNING: If the answer is
yes, this Skinny Rabbit could
possibly cause shortness of life.
See Exodus 20:12.)*

7. GS: ❑ Does _____
honor your parents or draw
you closer to your parents?

SR = Skinny Rabbit

GS = Great Stag

8. SR: ❏ Does being with (or at, or doing) _____ cause you to feel bad toward, dishonor, or hate a person or group of people?

8. GS: ❏ Does being with (or at, or doing) _____ encourage you to value others—even those with different thoughts or backgrounds?

9. SR: ❏ Does being with (or with those at) _____ drive a wedge between a husband and wife? Does this person (or persons or place or activity) promote actions or policies that are destructive or insensitive to home and family relationships? (For example, many company meetings with vendors are held at night, after you've worked all day, and they're held at restaurants that are really bars.)
(WARNING: If you checked this Skinny Rabbit box, you set off a Your-Marriage-Could-Easily-Go-Up-in-Smoke Detector. People, businesses, or situations that require people to choose an environment that drives a wedge between a husband and wife are deep pits on the trail of this Skinny Rabbit. If you checked this box, don't minimize the danger. Deal with it right now.)

9. GS: ❏ Does this person (or place, or activity) _____ help you build, deepen, and strengthen your marriage, or the prospect of a God-honoring marriage?

SR = Skinny Rabbit

GS = Great Stag

10. SR: ❑ Could (person, situation, or activity) _____ cause you to be dishonest or steal? (Yes, cheating on taxes is dishonest. Let's say you've always taken every single deduction you could legally take and also reported all your income. But this person or company makes a lot of cash transactions and doesn't report anything close to the amount actually earned. Now you're on her team or his tax return. Not reporting what you should is stealing, any way you look at it. People or companies that cut legal corners should get a quick Skinny Rabbit check mark.)

10. GS: ❑ Does _____ encourage you toward honesty and generosity?

11. SR: ❑ Does _____ lie or spread rumors about other people?

11. GS: ❑ Does _____ strive to tell the truth even if it costs him or her? Does he or she try to avoid tearing down others?

12. SR: ❑ Does being with _____ motivate you to make constant comparisons with other people's positions, possessions, or spouses?

12. GS: ❑ Does _____ seem grateful for what he or she has and rejoice when others succeed?

SR = Skinny Rabbit

GS = Great Stag

13. SR: ❏ Is _____ proud or cocky? Does this person put others down or refuse to admit any wrongdoing? *(CAUTION: If you check this box, you may be headed toward a new season in your life: fall. See Proverbs 16:18.)*

13. GS: ❏ Is _____ secure in who he or she is without putting others down? Is this person humble, even if very successful?

14. SR: ❏ Would you consider _____ to be a "Martha" (busy-busy in the kitchen, shop, or office, but forgetting the important things. Someone who puts urgency before importance)?

14. GS: ❏ Would you consider _____ to be a "Mary" (someone who has a sense of what's really important, putting importance before urgency)?

15. SR: ❏ Does _____ want to be alone all the time, or resent your spending time with good friends? (Does this person dislike your friends? Does he or she become jealous if you want to spend time with a friend?)

15. GS: ❏ Does _____ encourage you to maintain healthy relationships with good friends? Does this person have other strong friendships too?

16. SR: ❏ Does _____ cause you to be depressed, inward focused, or angry toward yourself or others?

16. GS: ❏ Does _____ cause you to be joyful and thankful?

HOW TO IDENTIFY YOUR SKINNY RABBIT

SR = Skinny Rabbit

GS = Great Stag

17. SR: ❏ Are rules to _____ more like optional suggestions? Does this person or organization feel that crossing legal or ethical or agreed boundaries is OK as long as you don't get caught? *(CAUTION: If ethics are optional, how can you know that this person or organization's commitment to you is real or that promises carry any weight?)*

17. GS: ❏ Does _____ help you stay *between the lines* in doing what's right and respect legitimate rules and authority? That doesn't mean that one who gets an occasional traffic ticket or jaywalks is a scofflaw. But does this person make a serious, consistent effort to honor laws and rules?

18. SR: ❏ Is _____ self-centered? Or does this person (organization or activity) tend to make you self-centered?

18. GS: ❏ Is _____ other-focused? Or does this person (organization or activity) help you to focus on others instead of yourself?

19. SR: ❏ Does _____ take without giving anything back?

19. GS: ❏ Does _____ give without expecting anything in return?

20. SR: ❏ Is _____ a quick fix for a damaged or broken relationship or problem situation you've recently experienced?

20. GS: ❏ Does being or staying with _____ make long-term sense? Have you been in this relationship long enough to really know? Long enough to evaluate it in different seasons and settings?

21. SR: ❏ Does _____ tend to have bad relationships with others? Do others have low opinions of this person, company, or situation?

21. GS: ❏ Does _____ tend to have excellent relationships with others? Do others hold this person, company, or situation in high esteem?

It's Time for the Bonus Round!
You're almost finished! Only the Bonus Round remains. This round alone may tip the scale one way or the other.

SR = Skinny Rabbit   GS = Great Stag

SR: Do any of the following mind-sets characterize _____ ?

GS: Do any of these positive mind-sets characterize _____ ?

(Score 1 point for each description checked.)

(Score 1 point for each description checked.)

SR = Skinny Rabbit	GS = Great Stag
☐ Apathetic	☐ Big-hearted
☐ Blabber-mouthed	☐ Caring
☐ Blame-shifting	☐ Confident
☐ Cynical	☐ Courageous
☐ Deceptive	☐ Diligent
☐ Destructive	☐ Discerning
☐ Fantasy-minded	☐ Edifying
☐ Fearful	☐ Heart-conscious
☐ Gullible	☐ Hopeful
☐ Image-conscious	☐ Humble
☐ Impulsive	☐ Kind
☐ Lazy	☐ Levelheaded
☐ Lowly Thinking	☐ Obedient to Rules
☐ Prideful	☐ Responsible
☐ Problem-focused	☐ Slow to speak
☐ Rebellious	☐ Solution-focused
☐ Shortsighted	☐ Thoughtful
☐ Small-minded	☐ Truthful
☐ Unkind	☐ Visionary
_____ Total points	_____ Total points

WHAT'S THE SCORE?

Add up the Skinny Rabbit column, and then add up the Great Stag column. Is this person, possession, position, promotion, or place more Skinny Rabbit or more Great Stag? The next important question: Now that you know, what steps are you going to take?

If you find that you are clearly on the trail of a Skinny Rabbit, or even caught in a bog, you may be tempted to do nothing at all. After all, the reason you pursued the rabbit was that it seemed attractive. We're naturally reluctant to give up things that attract us. To justify staying on the trail you may be tempted to blame the test: "Oh, that score means nothing. How did they construct this test anyway? Is it standardized? Who are they to judge my choices? It's my life, and I should live it as I please."

The pit looms dark and deep, just ahead.

Now is the time to start becoming a Wise Hunter. Don't try to make excuses. The first step may well be to seek the counsel of a wise friend, mentor, or pastor to help you find your way off the Rabbit Trail and back on the track of a worthwhile goal.

One place you can always find a Wise Hunter is in the book of Proverbs. We've already quoted from Proverbs many times in this book. That's because it's a book filled with Wise Hunter advice for identifying and avoiding Skinny Rabbit Trails. For example, whenever in this book you see the word *foolish*, *simple*, *wicked*, *faithless*, *lazy*, or *sluggard*, think *Skinny Rabbit*. On the other hand, when you see *wise*, *righteous*, *upright*, *faithful*, or *diligent*, think *Wise Hunter*.

Once you've caught the concept, you'll start seeing it pop up in all kinds of Scripture. For example, you'll see it in God talking to His people, the Israelites:

> *I have set before you life* [Great Stag Trails]
> *and death* [Skinny Rabbit Trails],
> *blessings* [Great Stags] *and curses* [Skinny
> Rabbits]. *Now choose life* [the Great Stag],
> *so that you and your children may live.*
> —Deuteronomy 30:19

And you'll see it when Paul addresses his friends in Corinth:

> *Everyone who competes in the games goes into*
> *strict training. They do it to get a crown that*
> *will not last* [Skinny Rabbit]; *but we do it to*
> *get a crown that will last forever* [Great Stag].
> *Therefore I do not run like a man running*
> *aimlessly* [down a Skinny Rabbit Trail].
> —1 Corinthians 9:25–26

It's not easy to cope with finding the truth about the

Skinny Rabbit you may have been chasing. But only the truth can keep you out of bogs and pits, and only the truth can free you from them once you've fallen. So it's vital that you detect those Skinny Rabbit Trails early, and either stay off of them entirely or get off immediately.

WHAT'S YOUR SKINNY RABBIT STORY?

If you have identified your Skinny Rabbit, the whole team here at StrongFamilies.com would love to hear your story. I can't promise to respond to every e-mail personally or that we can post every Skinny Rabbit e-mail on the Web site. But I can promise that we'll read carefully

every single e-mail and pray for those who may have gone too far or too long down a Skinny Rabbit Trail. E-mail us at StrongFamilies@aol.com.

I've provided the space below for you to identify the Skinny Rabbit you've been following. It will help you to clarify your direction and understand the needs that led you astray.

MY SKINNY RABBIT STORY

_____

_____

_____

_____

_____

_____

_____

I am happy to tell you that no matter what Skinny Rabbit Trails you've been on, there's a way to turn around and head in a productive direction. So don't give up or be discouraged if you could write pages, not just paragraphs, on all the trails you've been down. Identifying your Skinny Rabbit is the first step to stop following it and to get back to your true path.

11
GETTING OFF A
SKINNY RABBIT TRAIL

Let's take a final look at our friends, Elmer and Eloise Smudley. Remember that we left them running rampant down several Skinny Rabbit Trails that had the whole family in a busy-tizzy frenzy that finally crashed into chaotic rubble.

Elmer and Eloise were emotionally deep-fried. They desperately needed some time off—some *be still* time. But ironically, they were too busy to find time not to be busy. Finally, after their disastrous Thursday-night meltdown, Elmer decided enough was enough. They were more than ready to stop chasing those Skinny Rabbits.

One week later, Elmer and Eloise somehow found time to get away to a little rental cabin in the middle of the woods. As they sat by the fireplace, far away from phones and obligations and stress, they talked through their impossibly busy lifestyle.

They pulled out their handy Skinny Rabbit Detector

to evaluate their friends, their activities, their possessions, their mind-sets, their dreams, and lots more. As
they went down the list of activities, obligations, and
people they were involved with, they asked God, "Is this
a Skinny Rabbit or Great Stag Trail?" Elmer was partic-
ularly shaken by what he discovered when he poured
Paula's Pickles through the Skinny Rabbit Detector.

By the end of the weekend, Elmer and Eloise decided
together to jettison some things from their lives—even
some very worthwhile things—so they could focus on
the most important things, which was each other and the
kids. They also decided to back away from some Skinny
Rabbit friends. And Elmer started praying about his job
in a different way than ever before.

Some of their decisions were painful, but they bit
the bullet and made them. The result was that over the
next few weeks they felt their load lift, and they lived
out the truth of what Jesus said:

> *Take my yoke upon you and learn from me,*
> *for I am gentle and humble in heart,*
> *and you will find rest for your souls.*
> *For my yoke is easy and my burden is light.*
> —Matthew 11:29–30

One night, while catching up on some work during
the late hours, Elmer overheard Eloise laugh. It was a

little thing, but to him it was big because he hadn't heard her laugh in a long, long time. Far too long. It was a wonderful, musical sound to his ears.

The next day at work, Elmer leaned back in his executive chair and looked out his executive window at the clouds changing shapes on a bright blue canvas. He glanced back at Eloise and the kids smiling at him from the framed photo on his executive desk. Bobby and Betsy had changed a lot since this photo was taken. When was that? Three years ago. Wow. They had found no time to sit down for a family picture since then.

As Elmer gazed at the picture, he realized that the kids were growing up, but he barely saw them anymore except for a few moments during occasional week-ends. He had promised Bobby a trip to a baseball game, but work had taken up all his weekends lately. He was going to take Betsy out shopping at the mall for some daddy-and-daughter time, but he'd had to postpone that too.

As he stared at the faded photo, a strange but frightening picture came into his mind. He saw himself years in the future as a withered old man, clutching this same photo, as his mind was haunted—not by deadlines and business reports, but by lonely regrets.

Ring. His phone jolted him out of the little horror movie in his mind.

Ring. He started to reach for it.

Ring. And then something unusual happened. He stopped, his hand hovering in midreach.

Ring. Every instinct in his body told him to answer the phone.

Ring! His hand remained poised. The phone seemed to scream at him.

Ring!! What are you doing?! Don't just sit there—answer me! Now! You have to answer! Don't you hear me?! *Ring!!!*

And then . . . silence. Beautiful silence. The urgency evaporated. The moment had passed, and Elmer withdrew his hand. Something more important was stirring. He thought back to that little cabin in the woods, and he remembered something he hadn't seen in a long, long time. Eloise's animated sparkle—the life in those beautiful blue eyes—was back again. He remembered her laugh.

It occurred to him that if he didn't make a change soon, that sparkle would disappear again. The laugh would fade.

A radical thought began to emerge in Elmer's head. The director of the Junior Business Clinic had recently left to take another job. And now Elmer was thinking over what looked like a stupid career move. His salary would be half what it now was. But something inside him whispered that this was actually a Wise Hunter opportunity. He and Eloise had already talked it over. At the cabin she had reminded him how enthused he was about mentoring the kids at the clinic. On the issue of salary, she pointed out that they were now out of debt, which gave them the option to take on something like this. Something this radical.

The clouds in the photo blurred. Elmer wiped something from his eyes. He shook his head. And he smiled. He looked around at his executive office. Mahogany wood. Black marble. Polished brass. Skinny Rabbit stuff.

True, he felt a pang of fear, but it was quickly overcome by a swelling wave of excitement. He ignored the blinking message light on his phone and snatched his jacket off the brass coat rack. He paused at the door and took one last look at the office. Then he turned off the light, and all the colors in it faded to shadows of gray and black.

Except for Thursday nights, Elmer had always trudged up the front steps of his home at about eight or nine o'clock when the kids were going off to bed or already tucked in. But this evening, for the first time in years, he arrived home at five and full of energy.

He bounded up the front steps and paused. A warm light glowed from the front window—Bobby was playing checkers on the floor with his mom. Eloise pretended to look shocked as Bobby scored a triple jump. Bobby giggled. In the corner Betsy was playing tea party with her entire stuffed bunny collection while special guest, Toodles the Poodle—decked out in a bright print bonnet—licked one of the teacups.

Elmer smiled, turned the knob, opened the door, and became a Wise Hunter, setting his feet on the path of the Great Stag.

12
A FEW FINAL
THOUGHTS

Whether you are *on* a Skinny Rabbit Trail or you *are* a Skinny Rabbit leading someone else to a dead end, you can change. This is true no matter how far down a Skinny Rabbit Trail you've gone, or what pits and bogs have trapped you along the way. You have a choice, just like Becky. And just like the Smudleys.

You can choose to get off of that futile trail. You can get out of that pit. You can choose to surround yourself with Wise Hunters—people who think long-term, who work hard at living lives of faithfulness and produce the fruit that shows it. Look for these people—friends, pastors, mates, and associates to come alongside you and keep you on the path of purpose. They are out there. And they're willing to help when you make the effort to reach out.

When you do team up with Wise Hunters, you'll put yourself on the path to becoming a Wise Hunter yourself. You will be amazed at how living a Wise Hunter life fills you with hope. Living such a life offers you a future filled with all the potential God intended. Not full of busyness—that's Skinny Rabbit stuff—but full of God's power, full of His life in you, full of His purpose worked through you.

Finally, let me leave you with encouragement gleaned from God's own words as you seek Him and His path for you:

Trust God—He will lay out the path before you.

> *Trust in the LORD with all your heart*
> *and lean not on your own understanding;*
> *in all your ways acknowledge him,*
> *and he will make your paths straight.*
> —Proverbs 3:5–6

He will guide your steps.

> *In his heart a man plans his course, but*
> *the LORD determines his steps.*
> —Proverbs 16:9

Don't mess with Skinny Rabbit Trails.

> *Do not swerve to the right or the left;*
> *keep your foot from evil.*
> —Proverbs 4:27

A FEW FINAL THOUGHTS

Don't worry for anything along the way. Keep your focus on God.

> *But seek first his kingdom*
> *and his righteousness, and all these*
> *things will be given to you as well.*
> —Matthew 6:33

Keep heading toward the light.

> *The path of the righteous is like the first*
> *gleam of dawn, shining ever brighter*
> *till the full light of day.*
> —Proverbs 4:18

Do all these things and you'll become a Wise Hunter, sure to win the prize at the end of your journey.

NOTES

Chapter 5
Are You on a Rabbit Trail?
1. Robert Smith, e-mail communication to author, December 1, 2006.

Chapter 6
Bogs, Pits, Swamps, and Caves
1. www.soulkerfuffle.blogspot.com/2006/10/view-from-top.html.
2. Martin Seligman, "Staying happier for longer," BBC News, http://news.bbc.co.uk/1/hi/programmes/happiness_formula/4903464.stm.

Chapter 8
Wise Hunters to the Rescue
1. John Kasich, *Courage Is Contagious* (New York: Doubleday, 1998), 233.
2. George Bennard, "The Old Rugged Cross," 1913.

Chapter 9
Learning to Be Still: The Key to Following the Path of Peace
1. Mary Ann Bird, "The Whisper Test," *Guideposts Magazine*, January 1985.

ABOUT THE AUTHOR

John Trent, PhD, is president of The Center for Strong Families and StrongFamilies.com, which has become a leading family-enrichment community committed to strengthening marriage and family relationships worldwide. Dr. Trent speaks at major conferences and provides follow-up materials for churches, small groups, and couples. He is also a nationally renowned author whose books have won two Gold Medallions and have been chosen many times as Gold Medallion finalists. His award-winning and best-selling books include *The Blessing*, *The Two Sides of Love*, and *The 2-Degree Difference*. John has been a featured guest on radio and television programs such as *Focus on the Family*, the *700 Club*, and CNN's *Sonya Live*. John and his wife, Cindy, have been married for more than twenty-five years and have two daughters, Kari and Laura.

More from John Trent

JOHN TRENT, PH.D.
GARY SMALLEY

MORE THAN ONE MILLION COPIES SOLD

The
BLESSING

GIVING THE GIFT of UNCONDITIONAL
LOVE AND ACCEPTANCE

0-7852-6084-6

A timeless bestseller with more than one million copies sold, this book has helped individuals, parents, families, and small groups learn to give and receive the life-changing gift that the Bible calls *the blessing*.

The unconditional love and approval that come with the blessing is vital to our self-esteem and emotional well-being. *The Blessing* is a must-read for you and your family.

To join an online community of people committed to giving the blessing and to find out about an online, interactive course created by Dr. Trent, please visit:
www.TheBlessing.com.

And for couples

Be sure to pick up *Love Is a Decision: Proven Techniques to Keep Your Marriage Alive and Lively*—another national bestseller from Dr. Trent.

When you're in love, the sun shines brighter, and the birds sing sweeter. You feel warm and happy inside. But what happens when the chemicals subside and the feelings wane? When dissappointments accumulate and conflicts grow deeper, what motivates you to stay and work it out? Discover the answer in *Love Is a Decision* and learn the art of meaningful conversation, the secret of a close-knit family, and how to energize your mate in sixty seconds! 0-8499-4268-3

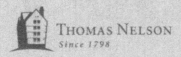

THOMAS NELSON
Since 1798

ADVANCED COACHES TRAINING

If you, or anyone else at your church are interested in using this DVD series to help launch a cutting edge marriage and family ministry at your church, then sign up for the StrongFamilies Advanced Coaches Training! This training is a three day event and takes place in beautiful, Scottsdale, Arizona. Included in this training is pre- and post-class mentoring, the Leading From Your Strengths Class 200 training kit, and practical, personalized attention from our experienced staff. Our Advanced Coaches Training topics include:

- Starting an ongoing marriage and family ministry at your church
- Be part of our Innovation Alliance
- Leading From Your Strengths (advanced training)
- "Coffee Cup" coaching and referral training
- Living The Blessing
- Life Mapping
- Story Boarding
- Skinny Rabbits
- 2 Degree Difference

To sign up, log on to our website and click on the Advanced Coaches Training link or call Jeff Thibault our Director of Operations and Training at 480-718-3040.

The Center for StrongFamilies
8283 N. Hayden Rd. Suite 258, Scottsdale, AZ 85258
Phone: 480-718-3040 • strongfamilies.com
E-Mail: moreinfo@strongfamilies.com

Printed in the USA
CPSIA information can be obtained
at www.ICGtesting.com
LVHW031211080823
754129LV00002B/3